RON BARTSCH

THE CORONA DILEMMA

20-20 THINKING FOR THE NEXT NORMAL

Copyright © 2021 Ron Bartsch

ISBN: 978-1-922409-39-3
Published by Vivid Publishing
A division of Fontaine Publishing Group
P.O. Box 948, Fremantle
Western Australia 6959
www.vividpublishing.com.au

 A catalogue record for this
book is available from the
National Library of Australia

CONTENTS

INTRODUCTION

By Colette Smith

What is creativity? To most people, creativity is a term often reserved for those in artistic fields, for those talents that appear from the outside to be bestowed upon a fortunate and select few who entertain and move us through the use of words, fine arts, music, dance, and all those other fields your parents begged you not to pursue in college. The term is often thought of as something you're either born with or you're not, like blue eyes or O-negative blood type.

Worse still, this idea of a God-given talent for creativity has convinced generations of people into believing they don't have the capacity for generating creative ideas in their personal or professional lives.

"I'm just not that creative."

Wrong.

We're all creative, we're all born with the capacity to create. All we need is a little guidance.

Some linguistic theories suggest that we're all born with the capacity for language, that as humans, our brains will always have the ability to learn language. The specifics of the language are irrelevant, whether it's English or Xhosa or sign language or whatever it might be, it doesn't matter, our brains are just wired for it. However, we don't learn our first language in a bubble. As babies, we take in input from our surroundings, we experiment with making sounds and test the reactions, and as we grow, we build increasingly complex models of grammar and expanded vocabularies to do the thing our brains were innately wired to do.

Creativity is the same. Devoid of input and roadmaps and encouragement to experiment and try new things, we're not likely going to be all that great at it. It needs time. It needs practice. And it needs the kind of structured grammar of a language where it can explore the bounds within and push the boundaries beyond.

This book is one such language and one such set of grammar rules. It describes the why and the how of the language of creativity in such a way that any of us can learn it. But it takes time. It takes practice. It takes effort and deliberate, conscious action. Like learning any language, you won't be perfect at it immediately and the process might very well struggle along the way. But what it *will* do is introduce you to a world of possibilities for what's next, what's better, and what will make you a better person and the world better for it.

The COVID-19 pandemic absolutely blindsided us all, and its impact on our personal lives and on businesses around the world is undeniable. The life we knew before 2020 will likely never be the same. As individuals and as business leaders, we're sitting at the crossroads of something extraordinary and we're all being presented with two clear choices:

1. Should we continue on as before and try to replicate the pre-pandemic world within the constraints that a post-pandemic world will bring? Or
2. Should we take this unique opportunity to forge a new path, one not just built around the challenges of a post-pandemic world, but one that actively embraces the new environment we're now living in?

As the book will discuss in greater detail, our minds find far more comfort in the predictable and the known than in the unpredictable and unknown. In this book, Ron Bartsch calls this "frozen thinking," that kind of inability to think beyond what's existed and the fear inherent in thinking differently. Yet humanity depends on creativity to make it through the troubling times we're facing and to see an improved future on the other side. Whether these are small, personal changes in the way we conduct our lives or massive corporate or governmental changes that impact thousands of people and millions of dollars, the process remains the same, and the importance of creative thinking is equally imperative.

Tear It Down, Start Again

In the summer of 1950, following decades of Japanese occupation and years of internal civil conflict, the Korean War broke out between the north and the south of the country. The bloody war raged for three years, destroying infrastructure and homes, and killing and wounding millions of people on both sides of the newly drawn border that bifurcated the Korean peninsula.

In the decades that followed, South Korea oscillated between democratically elected leaders and a series of military coups and authoritarian dictators. However, through some forward-thinking policies and investments, inter-national economic treaties, and a lot of hard work, the country transformed from a developing country that had been all but completely flattened during the war to a developed country that today stands as the world's 12th biggest economy. To demonstrate how massive this turnaround was, in 2016, on average, globally, people were 4.4 times richer than they were in 1950 (as measured by GDP per capita). By comparison, South Koreans were 32 times richer than in 1950. Of course, many external factors and inter-national investment also played its part in this massive transformation – known as the Miracle on the Han – yet during the same time period, South Korea's economic turnaround was unmatched, leaving a legacy that serves as a model for other developing nations today.

Economists and historians may argue at length about why and how South Korea managed such a turnaround from being one of the poorest countries in the region to a world-leading economy. But ultimately, sometimes in order to build something great, you need to demolish the old and start again with renewed assumptions. South Korea as a nation took the opportunity that devastation and ruin had left them with, and rather than attempt to rebuild the country based on assumptions formed before the war or before Japanese occupation, they rebuilt it looking ahead at what the world looked like in the moment and how it would look in the future, and developed policies that would lay the groundwork for a brighter future. It wasn't always easy going and they most definitely did not always get it right. Under these authoritarian leaders, many Korean people suffered and fought hard for the freedoms that they enjoy today, and still, much work lies ahead. Yet, the lesson of South Korea is one worth remembering. As we trudge through the hell that is this pandemic and look at the destruction it has caused, we can take the opportunity to build something new for ourselves or our businesses. You won't always get it right but doing the same thing over and over again likewise won't get us out of the rubble either.

Making Change, One Chapter at a Time

This book is laid out in six chapters, although it's probably better to look at it as five chapters with a sixth chapter that serves as ongoing support to the habits introduced in each chapter. Each chapter is structured with the intent of exploring how to make creative thinking part of your everyday life and business and delves into why the practice is so important. Chapter 6 also introduces a questionnaire that Ron has created and refined to provide a benchmark of your current state of creativeness. Ideally, the questionnaire is best taken before you launch into Chapter 1, and can be retaken at any time, but it's a good idea to take it again at the end or once you've started making progress on you creative thinking journey. As such, this book is intended to be read as follows:

Introduction

Chapter 6 introduction and questionnaire

Chapter 1 → Chapter 6 (habits 1 and 2)

Chapter 2 → Chapter 6 (habits 3 and 4)

Chapter 3 → Chapter 6 (habits 5 and 6)

Chapter 4 → Chapter 6 (habits 7 and 8)

Chapter 5 → Chapter 6 (habits 9 and 10)

Chapter 6 retest and conclusion.

Of course, you can approach the book any way you please, and if you think you'll get more out of it reading it sequentially, then absolutely give that a go.

In the interest of clarity, it's also worth going over a few terms and definitions used throughout the book. Although these are explained in greater detail in later chapters, having a broad understanding of them before jumping in will help synthesize the information and create a smoother reading experience.

Corona Event

We're all likely to face at least one corona event at some point in our lives. You may have already. The pandemic may be yours right now. Or perhaps in the years to come you'll face one. Maybe it's all of the above. Whatever the case may be, a corona event is a significant moment in your life that forces you to reevaluate how you've been doing things. Oftentimes these can be traumatic events, but not always.

To classify as a corona event, it needs to meet two conditions:

1. It needs to be a personally significant event that derails your normal life or way of doing things. This is the catalyst to derail your train of normality, a disruptor to your everyday life.
2. It needs to disrupt and/or isolate you away from the way you normally do things.

A corona event is likely to involve taking something away from your normal surrounds rather than adding something extra. For example: it's more likely to involve the breakdown of a relationship rather than the beginning of a new one, or the loss of a loved one rather than the birth of a child or, as Ron discusses in the book, in the midst of a global financial crisis rather than during a business's boom.

When your corona event happens, it gives you the opportunity, within your changed circumstances or environment, to reflect upon what has happened. It's during this time of reflection that you realize that perhaps the life you had been leading could've been better. Perhaps there are more worthy values that you'd prefer to uphold than those you're currently supporting.

You will read about Ron's corona event in Chapter 1. For me, my corona event was my father's death in 2018 that caused me to start considering where I was going in life. My husband and I had been living in San Francisco for several years where his career flourished while mine felt it had hit a dead end. I was frustrated, struggling to make friends, and utterly lost, paralyzed by concepts of what I "should" do and who I "should" be. When my father passed away suddenly, my husband and I rushed back to Australia, and after the funeral, I lingered behind while he returned to normal life back in the US. A couple weeks after the funeral, I went to South Korea for a kind of holiday-slash-remote-working-sojourn. I'd visited the country several times in the past and had fallen in love with its language, food, culture, and history, but this trip was different. This time I was completely and thoroughly alone in my grief, away from anything that even resembled normal life. I gave myself a kind of routine, setting myself up at a co-working space in a business district of Seoul, and worked remotely for three months. I took occasional trips around the country. I ate whatever and whenever I felt like. I cried and I drank soju and wrote half a novel and I went out clubbing until three or four a.m. I struggled. I survived.

About two months into the trip, when returning to some semblance of normal life had again crossed my mind, I idly started exploring things that interested me to see how I could face coming back to a life that I felt so dissatisfied with. I loved South Korea, despite (or perhaps because of) how completely different it was from my own upbringing and experiences. I had been on-and-off learning the language for a few years, but I had no idea how to make it something I could do permanently. I researched visa options and discovered that without at least a bachelor's degree, my hopes of experiencing anything even resembling a real life there with my husband were slim-to-none. I'd always loved learning and had wanted to get a degree for a long time, but, as life is wont to do, I never got around to it. "Life," as John Lennon once put it, "is what happens to you while you're busy making other plans." So, I started researching universities. I looked at universities in the United States, in Australia where the costs are more affordable to citizens, and universities around the world. At almost 40 years of age, I applied for a place and was accepted into one of Australia's top universities as a mature-age student where I could pursue my dreams of learning about South Korea and its language and its place in the Asian region.

And so, having experienced a corona event, now comes the corona dilemma.

Corona Dilemma

As is covered in more depth in Chapter 1, a corona dilemma arises following a corona event. It's the point where you've established that your life (or business) hasn't been doing what you'd hoped, you've reevaluated your goals and what's most important to you, and you're now faced with two choices:

1. Return to the way things were before the corona event
2. Choose a different path

If you look at the example of a post-war South Korea, their corona event (the Korean War) completely demolished everything that stood before. Even the concept of a *South* Korea was new. To return to old ways, as one may argue the North pursued, wouldn't meet the newly established goals and values of the new times and new nation. So, South Korea chose a different path.

For me, I could choose to return to San Francisco, go back to my job and continue on unsatisfied with the direction of my life, but in the comfort of the known. Or, I could take a risk, accept the university offer, return to Australia temporarily to study and to follow my dreams. The risks were many. I risked my relationship with my exceptionally supportive husband. I risked being out of my depth surrounded by fresh-faced young adults with minds more capable of ingesting the kind of onslaught of input and knowledge required for university life. And I risked financial hardship, leaving a stable job, apartment, and security in San Francisco for the student life in Sydney, with no job, expensive rent to pay as a student, and instability juggling life and relationships between the two countries.

A corona dilemma isn't a simple decision, but it is a vital one. As you'll see in the book, some well-known people and major corporations have also faced such a dilemma. Some preferred the safe option and found that playing it safe can also be risky, while others took the road less traveled.

I took the latter path. I accepted the offer, moved to Sydney, Australia, and am still working towards completing my degree. Beyond just the classroom, I've learned much more about myself during this time than I ever could've imagined. It's been a hard few years, made even harder during the pandemic, but I know in my heart of hearts that I made the right decision.

The thing with recognising and responding to a corona event is that it enables you to take control and ownership of the way you feel and act when experiencing the event. Society and those around us like to pass the situation off as "they're having a mid-life crisis" or "you're not your normal self at the moment," and so on. But what if who you are and what you've experienced and what you want to be is something that you have chosen? Perhaps corona events have always been happening but society and even those who love us most often don't like the idea of what the changed person is all about and hence label or mislabel the situation as a stage or mood or thing they're going through and they'll be "back to normal" soon. But one of the choices of the corona dilemma says there is no "back to normal."

20-20 Thinking

The corona event and subsequent corona dilemma are likely what brought you to where you are now. These are events or situations that lead to a conundrum that you need to resolve. 20-20 Thinking is a collection of models and tools you can apply to approach thinking creatively about the situation you're in. 20-20 Thinking is a part of the decision-making process that helps you connect remotely associated ideas to form new and creative ideas. It considers function rather than form in resolving problems. Broadly speaking, it's like the grammar of creative thinking. It gives you the bounds to play within and explore beyond.

The C-R-E-A-T-E Process

Ron has researched and developed a six-step guide that helps facilitate the creative thinking process. The process is explained in more detail in Chapters 3 and 4, but the six steps can be understood as follows:

C = Concept

This is the big picture without the detail. It's the idea that this thing needs to change, but not the specifics of how or when.

R = Raw materials

Within this are the three Rs of creativity: Recall (accessing pieces of information in your head), research (gathering data on those pieces of information) and reach out (sharing the information with others).

E = Elements

Elements are those elusive "ah-ha!" moments that happen when you bring together all the raw materials along with your past experiences to form a new idea. These "ah-ha!" moments are the building blocks for creative thinking.

A = Atmosphere

Creating the right atmosphere and environment conducive to allowing your mind to get creative is a crucial step in the process. Without this, your mind will struggle to think outside the box and make the creative connections necessary for devising new ideas.

T = Thought excursions

Thought excursions are a thinking process that occurs in the subconscious that facilitates joining the dots, and in turn, developing your concept.

E = Execution

Having new and creative ideas is awesome but are meaningless if they aren't executed. This final step is all about turning your creative concepts and ideas into reality.

Although I wasn't conscious of it at the time, my time in South Korea after my father passed away was spent going through this kind of process, albeit in a much messier, more disorganized manner. The beauty and simplicity of the processes and models Ron has researched and developed in this book is that they're largely intuitive, and almost even obvious. Yet, like getting from A to B, it's much quicker and far more efficient if you've got a road map in front of you rather than if you just wing it.

COVID Trauma

It's ok if you're not ready to take these steps yet. Living through a pandemic of this magnitude is a constant cycle of stress and for many, has been and continues to be highly traumatic. Some people have managed to cope by getting motivated, learning a language or baking sourdough or knitting sweaters or brewing beer or whatever it takes to pass the time productively. Not all of us find this kind of motivation and productivity in uncertain times, and that's ok too. Modern society has a habit of laying guilt on those who aren't capable of this kind of unbridled motivation at all times, and sadly, social media makes the burden of that guilt even heavier.

Even if you're not ready yet, it's ok. Don't beat yourself up for it. Read through the book and prime your body and mind for a time when you are ready to take in the complete message, and maybe along the way you find yourself more open to its ideas, models, and processes. Perhaps you integrate one new habit into your day or clear out a physical or mental space to prepare for future flights of creative fancy. Or maybe it's none of these. That's ok too. Go easy on yourself. If you don't come out of the other side of this pandemic fluent in Dothraki or having read *War and Peace*, remember that you've been attending to more important personal, psychological, and even financial needs that have taken up huge amounts of storage capacity in your mind.

That being said, try not to let this opportunity pass you by either. The coronavirus pandemic has been traumatic for us all, but it's also given us an opportunity to make a change in our life or business that rarely, if ever, comes about. Take hold of this chance. Use your corona event to launch yourself into a new normal on the other side of all this.

What to Expect When You're Expecting Change

I'm not going to lie, making the kind of changes this book is helping you make won't be easy. Big change isn't meant to be easy. The struggles and the pain, much like exercise, are part of the point – they're what make us stronger. Author Jennifer Wright tweeted in 2019, "People talk about caterpillars becoming butterflies as though they just go into a cocoon, slap on wings, and are good to go. Caterpillars have to dissolve into a disgusting pile of goo to become butterflies. So if you're a mess wrapped up in blankets right now, keep going."

In a speech to the United Nations in 2018, members of the South Korean pop group, BTS, spoke to delegates on the topic of owning one's individuality and developing a positive self-image. In the speech, one of the group's singers, Kim Nam-jun (also known by his stage name, RM) said:

"Yesterday's me is still me. Today I am who I am with all of my faults and my mistakes. Tomorrow I might be a tiny bit wiser and that would be me too. These faults and mistakes are what I am, making up the brightest stars in the constellation of my life. I have come to love myself for who I am, for who I was, and for who I hope to become."

This book is all about self-introspection, but that doesn't mean abandoning the person you once were. In fact, if we are to develop our next normal, we're going to need to look honestly and deeply into our past and the person we were so we can create the person we want to be and live the life we want to live. The following chapters are here to help you achieve the goal of living up to the person you know, deep down, you want to be and, indeed, should be.

Now, let's get started!

1

CHANGE IS OPPORTUNITY

"Intelligence is the measure of our ability to adapt to change."

Stephen Hawking

On leap year day, 2020, Britain's Prime Minister, Boris Johnson and his fiancée, Carrie Symonds, announced the joyful news that they were expecting their first child. Boris was elated and at an all-time personal high. Just five weeks later, the 55-year-old was in St Thomas' Hospital intensive care unit. He, along with millions of people around the world, had contracted the notorious coronavirus and was now fighting for his life. From a personal high to a fight for survival in a heartbeat, such is the indiscriminatory nature of pandemics.

We live in a world of change. And change, of whatever type, is inevitable. Some change can – and will – affect everyone, like the coronavirus has. Yet how we respond to change, as individuals and as corporations, is the most important aspect of change there is.

The COVID-19 pandemic is a crisis like nothing the world has seen before. While the globe groans under the weight of pain and suffering, stories of good and of hope abound. Out of the chaos, inspiring tales emerge of people helping others and spreading goodwill. From the high-rise apartment neighbors joining in chorus to serenade one another to the heartfelt applause in appreciation for healthcare workers, and the inspirational stories of everyday heroes and communities banding together, people are showing their kindness in unique and touching ways. Our isolation from the rush and bustle of everyday life has brought us closer together, and from the depths of despair comes hope, and from tragic endings come bright new beginnings.

The wake-up calls from reality, however, are never far from our minds. Waiting for us on the other side of this pandemic is a dramatically re-structured global economy and society. Old ways of thinking and the way things *used* to be are no use in the face of what's next. The new normal will require us to become more comfortable dealing with contradictions and ambiguity. The new normal is at our doorstep – it's up to us to decide how to answer its call.

Now, more than any other time in history, is the time to answer that call, to take hold of these unprecedented opportunities and forge your own path towards your next normal.

Here's what we need to do:
Let's approach life's challenges from a different perspective. No matter how insurmountable those challenges may seem, a new perspective will let us see things that were once clouded over and obscured from our view. What once seemed impossible can become viable options. By changing the way we look at the world, the world we look at changes.

The Corona Dilemma

A corona dilemma is a problem brought about by a significant event. Let's call this experience a corona event. This event compels us to make a determination as to what things in life are most important and what values are meaningful. For you, this corona event may be the coronavirus, but not necessarily. Perhaps your time in isolation may trigger your own corona event or reflect on recent changes in your life that spark a corona event. For me, it was an unplanned and completely unexpected assignment on the Pacific island of Vanuatu that completely changed the way I viewed my life and the world I had created around me. Until then I had been passing my time (and life) working in public service and in the belief that I was securing a carefree and satisfying future. Within weeks of arriving, shrouded in the tranquility of my modest hillside apartment, I began to ponder and reassess what in life was really important to me – my family and my relationship with my most precious soulmate of 20 years. In such idyllic surrounds, I wondered about what I wanted to do with the rest of my life and realized that for years I had been nurturing and protecting certain values that were, in fact, of little or no value. In no way were they going to make for a better life. So, I decided, there and then, to make a change for the better.

The corona dilemma arises because this decision involves a choice:

1. You can select the path of least resistance, go with the flow, and return to your normal world
   OR
2. You can choose to start doing things differently.

Figure 1: The Corona Dilemma

When I was in that apartment in Vanuatu, I could easily have succumbed to old habits and just recreated my old life in new surroundings. Instead, I took cues from my situation, and with a curious, open heart, I explored them. I learnt new things about myself and the world, and rather than just packing those discoveries away in my suitcase and returning home to the old normal, I made the conscious decision to carry these new-found values with me wherever life takes me. I would be forever changed. There was no going back. I *chose* to approach life differently with a new perspective. Yes, I faced challenges. For days on end I would doubt my decision and reimagine that perhaps my old normal really wasn't *that* bad after all. But this is where I got it wrong, and this is where *we all* get it wrong – we get sucked into believing in the sanctuary of security and falsely equating what is normal to what is secure. But this is an artifice. No amount of normality within your surrounds is going to save you from a life of misery if you are not at first secure in yourself. During those four short months in Vanuatu, I re-connected with my creativity and came to realize what was most important to me, and that was just the assurance I needed to take me into my next normal.

To do things differently (as opposed to doing different things) means your next normal may be much better than your old normal, but it *will* be different. The anxiety of this uncertainty only further contributes to our dilemma.

Your corona dilemma won't arise if you continue to do things the way you always have. If you follow the crowds, this future will not reveal its options. Changing *with* society, no matter how rapid and extensive that change may be, provides the comfort that our safety and security will be assured since we are still part of *our* society. We draw comfort from being part of the herd. However, the corona dilemma will <u>only</u> emerge if and when you start seeing the world differently.

20-20 Thinking

Our personal and distinct set of thought patterns often lead us astray, so we don't see things as they are, we see them as *we* are. For us to do things differently requires a shift in the way those patterns operate, initiated by a new way of thinking: 20-20 Thinking.

If you recall from the introduction, 20-20 Thinking is the ability to muster creative ideas by connecting remotely associated 'things' as part of our decision-making process. It considers function rather than form in resolving problems. It's similar to the way Steve Jobs approached the idea of using a touchscreen display for a cell phone and expanding that idea to include additional functions until it became the single source of entertainment and connecting with the world. The individual inventions and ideas around the iPhone already existed – touchscreen displays, cellular phone technology, applications, and everything else that makes up an iPhone. However, it was the confluence of all these ideas and technologies that made the iPhone such a revolutionary, life-changing product.

Following my corona event in Vanuatu, I also used 20-20 Thinking to map out my future. To work out how I was going to re-engage with my loved ones and land a job that really meant something to me, a job in which I could make a *real* difference rather than just going through the motions culminating in the inevitable public service retirement party, I used the 20-20 Thinking model to pull in ideas from all areas of my life. These weren't necessarily new ideas, but step by step, I pieced together a blueprint for a life I wanted and began to create my new normal that accommodated and protected my newly discovered values. As a result, within two months of returning home from my trip and putting that plan into action, I was appointed Head of Safety for Qantas Airways – the world's safest airline.

Breakthrough innovation or changing the way you live requires creativity, and creativity requires that you think differently about the way you think. Neuroscientists who study the way our brain works have discovered that innovators like Steve Jobs do think differently, but they use a technique available to all of us, what I refer to as 20-20 Thinking, that enables us to seek out and explore new opportunities that arise from a changed environment.

The world changed beyond recognition circa 2020 when pre-pandemic life-as-we-knew-it effectively ended. In our pre-virus world, we resisted the type of change that required any degree of reflective consideration. Sure, we love our smart phones, the internet, and social media, but all these changes to our daily lives were changes of least resistance. In fact, if we *didn't* adopt and adapt to these new things, we would most likely feel isolated and out of touch with society. Although our world has changed at an unprecedented rate over the past decade or so, the change we experienced and accepted was all part of the tsunami of technological enthrallment that irrevocably transformed our society. As all this change was part of society, we, being the social animals we are, accepted this as just being the norm.

However, the 2020 pandemic was different. The changes were immediate. It affected us all at around the same time, and it expected us to accept monumental changes to every aspect of our lives, livelihoods, businesses, and the world around us on a scale we'd never seen before. It forced us all to change or face then-unknown consequences to ourselves, our loved ones, and our community around us. It forced us to consider what was important and to change behaviors immediately, without warning, without notice.

On a national level, leaders around the world have had to reevaluate priorities, funding, and policy. They've had to close borders and rethink economies and balance competing issues around health, safety, the flow of capital, and freedoms that democratic nations normally take for granted. Companies large and small, with no advance notice, had to create new flexible work arrangements for employees so they could remain in business, and in many industries, immediately pivot to completely new ways of conducting business or face potential closure and financial ruin. On a personal level, we, the people, were left to pick up the pieces of the decisions made that were out of our hands. The way governments and businesses responded to the crisis were largely decisions we had to go along with. So, we too, had to change our daily habits and routines and develop coping strategies to deal with these immense, immediate changes going on in our lives.

While change may be the only real constant in life, human beings are evolutionarily predisposed to resist any change that requires us to think differently. This resistance may be based on some perceived fear of things that change, or of the anxiety of not conforming, or perhaps even an instinctive response to a more deep-seated human need. Irrespective of its origin, our antagonism to this type of self-initiated or individual change has become a societal norm – something that has been ingrained in most of us from a very early age.

In the wake of the pandemic, we've seen a lot of anger in different parts of the world targeted at decisions to close businesses and services that could pose serious health concerns for customers and employees. The anger has spilled into a particular domain of health and safety regarding wearing masks to curb the transmission of COVID-19. Many people have deeply struggled with this kind of individual, self-initiated change, and when facing a cavalcade of changes outside of their control, that anger, that antagonism against change, has spilled out. This is because change is fundamentally hard for us to internalize, and society has told us to avoid and rebuke this kind of sudden change time and time again.

By comparison, we didn't see these debates and bouts of anger in countries and regions for whom wearing masks was a part of daily life, say, to combat air pollution or fine dust particles. They had already internalized the practice and normalized it, so adding just one more thing to the list of reasons why wearing a mask in public spaces was a good idea was easy. They could just add it to what was already normal rather than completely changing their habits.

I have developed 20-20 Thinking as a simple and powerful thinking tool to help us negotiate the next normal, aka life after the pandemic. The approach provides a method for us to start thinking in ways that will support and promote a better way of living and for corporations to achieve goals while maintaining their redefined core values. But for us to make the decision to decide upon a different way of thinking we must first make a break from the way we have done things in the past – and this is not easy. I know it's not easy because I've lived it. But I also know that it *can* be done.

The Needs we Need

Crisis changes the balance of risk and reward. In normal times, we don't tend to make personal changes because we fear the risk associated with change. We typically consider the equation: is the potential gain achieved by changing sufficient enough to outweigh the risk of failure? In a crisis, the dynamic shifts dramatically and the real risk becomes that of doing nothing. During a crisis, our risk tolerance increases because we consider other alternatives as unacceptable. A crisis forces us to focus on the here and now. Everything else, no matter how much it's loved, how beautiful it is, or how much comfort it brings us, is discarded if it's not essential. If it doesn't help us survive, then what is its purpose?

With the coronavirus crisis, and crises generally, the prime motivator for our unquestioning acceptance of the massive changes thrust upon us is the fear or threat to our physical and emotional safety. The responses to the COVID-19 pandemic are an amplification of the dynamics that drive other social and ecological crises: the prioritization of one type of value over others. This is the reason behind the phenomenal support of the Black Lives Matter movement. In normal times, our reluctance to accept such personal change is based primarily on our emotional and esteem values associated with our fear of failure or doing something different from the populous. This is consistent with the model of the hierarchy of human needs developed in the early 1940s by prominent American psychologist Abraham Maslow.

Figure 2: Maslow's Hierarchy of Human Needs

Maslow's model explains how our lower-order needs, such as physiological and safety needs, must first be satisfied before we will concern ourselves with the higher needs like esteem and self-actualization. Before the onset of COVID-19, many of us were concerned with pseudo-values, such as 'will I receive my performance bonus?' or 'how am I going to lose those excess inches around my tummy?' But all that flies out the window when confronted with the anxiety of your own mortality.

Maslow's hierarchy of human needs provides a powerful model for understanding the large-scale psychological effects of the coronavirus. For many of us, the uncertain future of the effects of this virus weigh heavily on our minds, causing great anxiety. In terms of Maslow's model, why the coronavirus pandemic is such a unique and unprecedented event is the sheer degree and magnitude to which it has had the effect of simultaneously knocking us all off the perches of our higher-level human needs. This has happened virtually overnight and on a worldwide basis. None of us will worry about higher-level needs when we've got physiological and safety needs that we first need to satisfy.

But such events have happened to all of us in the past and well before the onset of the COVID-19 crisis. Life frequently has a habit of knocking us all down to lower levels of Maslow's pyramid, so why is the current situation so different?

The big difference is that we are now not alone. We're all facing great uncertainty *together*. It's not restricted to one country, region, community, family or individual, it's happening on a global scale. This means we can share our concerns and anxieties with each other and feel heard and understood. In compliance with social distancing and self-isolation requirements, we satisfy our immediate 'safety' needs, so this positions us all on the 'belongingness and love' level of Maslow's pyramid. This human need brings about the desire for us to feel fully and unconditionally supported by someone else and to provide such support and love to others during these difficult times. That's why nowadays when I'm on my daily jog, people smile or wish me a nice day as I pass by and I, too, will break my stride and take the time to chat with my old neighbors, Alice and John, who, so they informed me, both turn 90 this year.

Albert Einstein once said, "It's in the middle of difficulty that we find opportunity." And so, along with this positioning on the hierarchy of human needs arises the opportunity for each of us to change for the better. We now have the opportunity to change our ways in support of protecting the things that *really* matter to us and navigate the path toward our next normal.

The Two Types of Change

To better understand the unique situation we now face, we should consider two basic types of change: *inter*-personal change and *intra*-personal change. Understanding how these outer and inner forces work to erode our resolve for change can help us identify them when they arise and combat against them.

Change from outside forces

Inter-personal change is generally referred to as environmental change as it affects more than one person and includes societal and organizational change. This inter-personal kind of change is reactive and is what we have experienced with the COVID-19 pandemic. It doesn't require a change to the way we think but rather it reinforces the notion of our acceptance of common practices and ways within a community or an organization. These new practices often become habitual, like the widespread uptake of modern technology of our previous normal. We may feel forced into this kind of change from outside influences, perhaps from our communities, society, from familial expectations, or other institutions and organizations. Or we may feel coerced into accepting these changes, whether we want to adopt them or not. The populous readily accommodates inter-personal change and the changed environment can very quickly become the norm. The new standards we accept become the new values of our society or the culture within an organization.

We have seen how quickly people of the world have been forced into an entirely new way of life under the COVID-19 sanctions. Strong habits, personal freedoms, and our entire way of life has instantaneously been replaced with strict constraints regarding social distancing and self-isolation. We have collectively changed our behaviors as governments and officials order these changes with harsh penalties for those who fail to comply. This isn't new. There are plenty of other examples where we've changed our ways for fear of being caught. Consider today's societal standards in terms of wearing seat belts in cars, drink-driving, and smoking in public areas. Although there is a choice as to whether or not an individual or organization decides to comply with these new rules, the strictness of the related offences is usually a sufficient deterrent to ensure conformity and it quickly becomes the new social order.

It's interesting to note, however, the contrast in behavior and attitudes between countries that have applied the above sanctions. In some countries where the rules have not been strictly enforced, for example, wearing car seat belts in the United States, many people do not comply, so widespread acceptance is not achieved. In many US states, it remains socially acceptable not to comply, and in 16 states, a police officer cannot stop and ticket a driver for not wearing a seat belt. Even when officers do ticket drivers and passengers with non-compliance, the fines may be as little as US$10. As a result of these inconsistent and infrequently applied laws, state seat belt usage rates range from 67 to 97 per cent. Despite the proven safety benefits of wearing seat belts, according to the National Highway Traffic Safety Administration, 48 per cent of those killed in passenger vehicles in the US weren't wearing a restraint when they died. Compare this with Singapore where non-compliance can result in a $1,000 fine or imprisonment for up to three months. With compliance of over 99 percent for drivers, Singaporeans have accepted wearing seat belts as the new way of life.

There are important reasons other than the imposition of fines or penalties as to why people will so readily accept this type of societal change: it's the type of change that presents an unambiguous difference – it may be unpleasant but it's certain. Although it's the type of change that may create anxiety, that anxiety is spread across the community.

This is precisely the type of change that a corona event brings about. Yet, although a corona event gives us the opportunity to create our next normal, if the change you accept is of a societal nature, if you just go along with the crowd or with expectations placed upon you, then you likely won't create your new normal. *Your* next normal will be *society's* next normal, and the chances are it will look very similar to your previous normal.

Change from within

Intra-personal or individual change is proactive, self-initiated, and does not happen unless *you*, as an individual or as a corporation, are prepared to do something different. By way of an example to contrast the two types of changes, it's easy for salespeople to sell many items and many different types of items but it's more difficult to sell those items in a different way. To sell differently requires a different type of thought process. When faced with a corona dilemma you need to start thinking differently so you can devise strategies to protect your newly re-prioritized core values. These are the values that you have determined as being important following your corona event.

Societies and large corporations are good at societal and organizational change, but they struggle when it comes to doing things different, as opposed to doing different things. Consider, for instance, how some organizations seem incapable of embracing gender equality within the workplace. Glass ceilings remain an integral part of their corporate architecture. Notwithstanding anti-discrimination legislation that provides for equal opportunity in recruitment and remuneration, gaping gender discrimination is still rampant. Male-favoring bias has been prominent in many professions and industry sectors, but this does not explain why in our contemporary commercial environment, similar corporations can have vastly contrasting gender ratios in senior management roles. Take, for example, Google's 2020 Diversity Annual Report that revealed women only held a little over a quarter of leadership roles at the company globally. Whereas by comparison Netflix reported that women made up almost half of all leadership positions globally. Companies that genuinely support gender equality throughout their business have changed their fundamental corporate values. This is an example of 'change from within' in a commercial scenario – an indicative feature of a progressive organization.

At a personal level there are also many examples of the contrast between inter-personal change and intra-personal change. Look how swift personal habits have changed when smoking was prohibited in the workplace and other public places. People very easily changed their habit of where and when they would smoke but most were unable to break their habit of smoking. Likewise, during the pandemic look how quickly we have stopped shaking hands. The compulsion of making some form of physical greeting interaction remains, so we have replaced hand shaking with elbow tapping or some other creative gesture. Deep-seated personal values and attitudes are continually reinforced by the habits we practice. Certain intra-personal habits are still very difficult to break even after you have decided that you genuinely *want* to change.

American existential psychologist, Dr. Rollo May suggests, "now it is no longer a matter of deciding what to do, but of deciding how to decide." Deciding how to decide requires a conscious realization that you have a choice of how you will contemplate your future. If you want your next normal to be founded on your reassessed values and beliefs, then you must dictate your new decision-making process based on the primacy of these values and beliefs.

For corporations, this means redefining the company's core values and how they will conduct business. The best way to explore the opportunities that a changed environment presents is through the agility of creative thinking, and one of the core values of your personal or organizational new paradigm must be to adopt a creative mindset.

In our dramatically restructured society and economy, old assumptions and our old way of thinking won't deliver us to the next normal we need. But creativity will. To do things differently in our next normal, we must undertake a paradigm shift initiated by a new way of thinking. Those of us who have experienced a corona event now have stark clarity about what's important in life. For individuals, this means re-evaluating the things that matter to us and making choices that prioritize these values. For business leaders, this translates to a commitment to maintaining realigned core corporate values.

"If you don't change your beliefs, your life will be like this forever. Is that good news?" (*Douglas Adams*)

In his book *The Courage to Create*, Dr. Rollo May draws on his extensive clinical practice experience to explain how we can break out of old patterns.

> *"We are called upon to do something new, to confront a no man's land, to push into a forest in which there are no well-worn paths and from which no one has returned to guide us. This is what the existentialists call the anxiety of nothingness. To live into the future means to leap into the unknown, and this requires a degree of courage for which there is no immediate precedent and which few people realize."*

There are no precedents with the COVID-19 crisis. It takes real courage to break out of our settled mold. Dr. May advocates that "the opposite of courage in our society is not cowardice, it is conformity." The courage we require is achieved through confidence in our ability to create our next normal. The process we must follow is that of creative imagination brought about by an entirely new way of thinking. Applying 20-20 Thinking to any situation produces the kind of intra-personal or individual changes we need to make. This is how we can fully realize the opportunities that change presents.

What most individuals lack is the fortitude to cultivate their own creativeness. Creative people are those with the courage to proceed and the strength to overcome resistance, despite their self-doubt. Creative people also display a remarkable ability to tolerate, accept, and even embrace contradiction and ambiguity. Crisis pushes us out of our comfort zone and into our creative zone. We've seen this in the countless stories throughout the pandemic crisis of people in self-isolation returning to simple, creative pleasures like baking bread at home, learning to play an instrument, or dressing up in outlandish outfits to put out the trash. The COVID-19 pandemic can bring out the most creative in all of us and provide us with the opportunity to truly transform ourselves in a way that will ultimately lead to a more enjoyable and fulfilling life. But we first need to commit to personal change from within for this to happen.

Prominent psychologists, Abraham Maslow and Carl Rogers, believed creativity was one of the higher capacities of human beings. They thought that to nourish one's creativeness was to move in the direction of one's higher self. According to Maslow, being creative isn't a luxury, it's a necessity for all who strive toward individuation and self-actualization.

Dr. May agrees and insists that we must consider the creative process as representing the "highest degree of emotional health" and as the expression of normal people in the act of actualizing themselves. This higher-level change of self-actualization, which sits at the apex of Maslow's pyramid, requires individual contemplation. In some instances, this may result in behavior or actions that many would consider counter-social or even anti-social. In other words, doing things or behaving in a way that may be quite different to the way the masses or society would behave. But this is the type of change that the corona dilemma is all about. It's the type of change that requires a very different way of thinking, and it's the type of change with which we struggle, and often reject entirely.

I know how alienating it can be when you begin to put into effect your life changing strategies brought on by the resolution of a corona dilemma. This happened on me on my return from Vanuatu to my substantive public service position. When I informed close work colleagues of my decision to pursue a new career direction, these revelations that had effectively changed the entire trajectory of my life were met with indifference. It was as though I was 'letting the team down' in even contemplating an alternative to the well-trodden run to retirement.

"Ronny Bartsch what are you doing?" Colleagues would ask. But even when faced with this opposition, I remained resolute. I *had* to change. I had far too much at stake for me not to.

Despite the resistance to this type of change, it is now more important than ever for us, and the organizations we work for, to resist this bias and embrace individual or intrapersonal change. We need to become comfortable with ambiguity and contradiction. Due to social conditioning our natural tendency is to accept the status quo which inhibits our creative expression.

To counter the anti-creative habits we have all developed throughout life, we need to develop creativity-promoting habits. And this is easier said than done. This book is intended to be the catalyst for you to begin your journey of changing the way you think and in identifying habits that will support these personal changes.

This individual change, which is essential for our personal betterment, also needs to be driven across our entire economy. Consider the pre-2020 world of commerce. For years, corporations focused on cost control as the primary means of remaining competitive. However, the post-2020 business climate requires a change in the way we do business. Competition in the commercial sector is even more intense. For companies to survive and prosper, they must look beyond costs and rethink the entire way they manage. In this new world order, the next normal business processes will no longer be aligned or even constrained by rational analysis or linear processes. We now live in an era where technological life cycles are measured in months rather than years or decades. It seems the only accurate cliché about the future is that we can never predict, with any degree of certainty, what it will look like. COVID-19 is a case in point.

On a fundamental level, as companies move toward their next normal, they need to become more agile in responding to an increasingly unpredictable economy. The corporate change required for an agile transformation is indeed a cultural transformation. During the pandemic there have been many instances where organizations have been creative and responded to the needs of a world in crisis. Boutique beer brewing companies and distilleries are producing hand sanitizer and designer clothing manufacturers are churning out fashionable face masks. Traditionally it has always been more difficult for larger companies to respond with the same degree of agility. As we will see later in this chapter, the world's most profitable company of the '90s almost went bankrupt because it was practically incapable of cultural transformation. Businesses need to nurture innovation during a crisis and consider the opportunities a crisis may present and then how to harness a new way of thinking to respond to the changing landscape.

Frozen Thinking

Even in previous global crises and times of mass disruption to our societies, commonly held beliefs are often thrown into question, but invariably, the status quo remains. Toward the end of World War II, the United States detonated two atomic bombs over the Japanese cities of Hiroshima and Nagasaki indiscriminately killing over 200,000 men, women, and children. Shortly after the bombings, Albert Einstein proclaimed that the release of atomic power on the world "has changed everything except our way of thinking." In the aftermath of traumatic events, life eventually return to normal and the status quo continues. Will this be the fate of the world in our post COVID-19 era?

As a challenge to Einstein's proclamation, Edward de Bono – physician, psychologist, author, inventor, and philosopher – in the opening sentence of his book *New Thinking for the New Millennium* posed the question: "Is it too late to change the way of thinking?" After fundamental societal change, we must ask the question: Why do we persevere with our old way of thinking when the opportunity to do things much, *much* better exists? There is a simple answer and it seems to all come down to our paradigms.

Our personal paradigms dictate the way we think and how we process information. These thought processes filter reality based on the opinions and values we have adopted through life's experiences. Psychologists use the term "frozen thinking" or "dogmatic cognition" to express our tendency to process information in a manner that reinforces our own personal beliefs, experiences, and expectations. This means that the thinking processes we applied in our pre-COVID-19 world will be the same and accompany us on our journey to our next normal unless we make the decision to change the way we think.

To better understand the workings of 20-20 Thinking, we first need to consider how our minds process information. When our conscious minds are busy and preoccupied, we're unable to fully explore our thoughts and develop new ideas. Smartphones, tablets, PCs, and all manner of technological devices have a tendency to occupy our minds in increasingly intrusive ways that put our minds in 'closed mode' where our thoughts are frozen. But when our conscious mind is switched off when we're, say, taking a shower, dreaming, gardening, self-isolating, or some other similar activity, we turn to 'open mode' and ideas tend to rise to the surface. When we're not otherwise preoccupied with our thoughts, the door to the cage opens and our minds fly away in unpredictable directions and land on a creative solution.

American astronomer and renowned author, Clifford Stoll, believes that what "turns the gears in our brains" isn't information, but rather ideas. Our minds think with ideas, not information. Albert Einstein, arguably the most creative individual of the twentieth century, said that words were "clunky". The creative process, by its very nature, does not lend itself to being explained merely by words. Albert believed that concepts and ideas are far more conducive to being visualized rather than expressed in words. This is how he came up with his breakthrough insights that led to the development of his theory of general relativity. Creative ideas emerge from learning to think differently – that's why we need to engage in 20-20 Thinking.

20-20 Thinking requires you to think in pictures through the practice of what I call *thought excursions*. This allows you to travel faster and further in your creative imaginings. Like Einstein, your thinking can leap universes. Thought excursions involve setting up a scenario in your mind and seeing how it plays out. The three-dimensional model espoused in this book is designed to stimulate your creative thinking and is the foundation of the 20-20 Thinking process.

The objective or outcome of processing any information is to generate concepts or ideas, which in turn results in the acquisition of knowledge. But when we process information in a more innovative manner, we come up with creative ideas. A whole world of possibilities and opportunities suddenly become significantly enhanced. Options become apparent and even the seemingly impossible become plausible alternatives. By changing the way we process information we change the way we see the world. We see the world in a different light, and we see it from a different perspective.

Success for companies in the post-COVID-19 era is now even more dependent upon the promotion of creativity and innovation. Business leaders often hail these as the most important enablers for the restoration of our economy, and over the past few decades, creativity and innovation have become the primary engine of growth for dynamic companies, surpassing raw materials, labor, and capital as the key economic drivers. Creative companies, or more specifically, companies who proactively seek and seize opportunities, aren't creative because it's prescribed in their constitutions. They're creative because of the people who run them and those who create or influence the corporate culture. Walter Isaacson in his biography, *Steve Jobs*, explains how this happened at Apple.

> "At a time when societies around the world are trying to build digital-age economies, Jobs stands as the ultimate icon of inventiveness and applied imagination. He knew the best way to create value in the 21st century was to connect creativity with technology, so he built a company where leaps of the imagination were combined with remarkable feats of engineering."

Creativity is also necessary when trying to restructure our personal lives. Our next normal may be far removed from the pre-pandemic world we once knew. So, to make sense of the life-*after*-the-pandemic world, we need to come to terms with the potential ramifications of all this change and seize the opportunities that change affords. Almost every day, somewhere on the planet, some new invention is born, or a zany new craze goes viral, and overnight a multi-million-dollar business is created. A kid in a college dorm with high-speed internet access has a good idea, starts a company, and in a couple of years is a billionaire. Facebook, Google, YouTube, Twitter, Instagram: it's a brave new and unpredictable world out there.

Never, in the history of civilization has there been a time of greater or more expedient access to information. Consider today's rate of accumulation of scientific knowledge. In 2019 there was an estimated 2.9 million scientific papers published. That's some 8,000 a day, or one published on average every 10 seconds. Our internal evolutionary processors are incapable of keeping pace in absorbing this amount of information and with the accompanying changes that transpire. Yet with such wealth of information at our fingertips, individuals and organizations alike must now seriously reflect on what to do with all of this knowledge and work out how to turn it into the kind of change we want to see in ourselves, in our businesses, and in the world around us.

Managing Change Beyond 2020

So, how do we best make that next career-progressing move, improve the quality of relationships, or better manage our personal affairs? How can organizations and the people who run them ever hope to stay ahead of the curve in these changing times? Upon what basis can we develop new marketing strategies and create financial models for growth forecasts and future investment? What is the answer?

The answer is that it's all about change, or more precisely, it's about how effectively we manage change. For organizations and individuals, the ability to readily adapt to a changing environment has now become the most important factor that dictates our future. Without change there is no medium for improvement or innovation or creativity. It's those who *embrace* change that are best placed to manage the change that's inevitable in our next normal. Manage change effectively and you effectively manage the future. We should be neither afraid nor deterred by this challenge but rather see change for what it is.

Change is the medium by which the opportunities of the future are presented. And *creativity* is the matrix against which adaptability to change is measured and achieved. By learning how to become creative and harness that power, then, and only then, can one change for the better.

Irrespective of whether you're contemplating a commercial decision or you're struggling with a personal issue, the most important factor influencing the decision-making processes is our rapidly changing environment. When properly applied, effective change management principles enable organizations and individuals to better adapt to change and become more agile in our decision making. This allows us to consider alternatives and explore opportunities that wouldn't otherwise have been apparent or that we would've previously considered too risky. What we need to appreciate is that it's not *change* that's risky but rather it's poor management that poses the biggest risk. If businesses and individuals don't manage change efficiently and effectively then they will most likely have to live with its unintended, and quite often undesired consequences.

Contrary to popular consensus, embarking on creative decision-making need not be fraught with danger. Neither creative nor conservative decisions have a direct correlation with risk. Risks are intrinsically associated with hazards, not decision-making. Hazards in this sense are anything that can have an impact on achieving personal goals or corporate objectives. On the other hand, decisions that have considered all relevant environmental hazards, including those that have arisen from the changed environment, must be superior decisions to those that have not, particularly when measured against the achievement of goals. These environmental hazards, from a corporate perspective, include technological advancements or the entry of new competitors in the market. On a personal level, hazards may include the impact of a change of employer or increased repayments on a mortgage or loan. There is, however, a direct correlation between superior decisions and creative decisions because creative decisions necessarily consider new ideas and new possibilities, both of which are stimulated by a changing environment.

To highlight this point, consider how Eastman Kodak, the global leaders in photographic technology and film for the better part of the 20th century, responded to a changed environment. When Kodak engineer, Steve Sasson, invented the first digital camera in 1975, the company had an opportunity to lead the digital photography revolution. But the company blew its chance because it failed to effectively manage a changed environment. Sasson later recalled, "it was filmless photography, so management's reaction was, 'that's cute—but don't tell anyone about it.'" The board and senior executives of Kodak failed to perceive digital photography as a disruptive technology and massively lost out in the end.

Former Kodak vice-president, Don Strickland, remembered, "We developed the world's first consumer digital camera, but we could not get approval to launch or sell it because of fear of the effects on the film market." Kodak's senior management was so focused on protecting their core business that they completely overlooked the hazards associated with not getting into the digital market. As a result, the company missed the digital revolution that they had, in fact, started. Then, in 2012, Kodak filed for bankruptcy.

Often the riskiest decisions are those that appear to be the safest. These conservative decisions are mostly based on precedent – how things have been done in the past according to how we perceive the world around us. But as we proceed to the next normal, there are no precedents to follow. The societal norm or play-it-safe option is the outcome we arrive at when we revert to frozen thinking. Non-creative organizations that continue to follow their ways of the past invariably fail. On the other hand, organizations that manage change effectively seize new opportunities when presented, and they succeed. Effectively managing the changes happening in our environment and taking assessed and acceptable risks, particularly as we sit at the precipice of a new post-COVID world, is the best, and perhaps only way to ensure our new normal won't just be a bad replication of the old normal.

Applying fundamental change management principles allows us to identify hazards that arise from a changed environment. We can then individually risk-assess the hazards and consider it against our appetite for risk. This works not just in the world of commerce but also in our personal lives. What's considered acceptable risk will vary but the facts remain: those who can more accurately and expediently assess a changed environment will gain over those who have been unable, unwilling, or unmotivated to consider fully the landscape of the new normal.

This is not a book on change management – there are many worthwhile publications that address that topic. I raise this issue to emphasize that the people and organizations who are focused on the nature and impact of change are better positioned to make appropriate creative decisions. This is because they have based their decisions considering the new environment that has been created, like, for example, the COVID-19 crisis, instead of the way the environment once was. As we move toward our next normal, it doesn't matter whether these decisions are commercial or personal in nature as the changed environment affects all facets of society.

The first global financial crisis of the new millennium made a massive impact on society affecting businesses and individuals alike. It affected all commercial and personal decisions relating to investments as new and unique hazards associated with the changed environment had, in most instances, not been fully considered. Financial institutions had been increasingly lending money to borrowers who had less than prime credit histories. An environment of easy credit and the upward spiral of home prices made investments in higher yielding subprime mortgages look like a new rush for gold. The US Federal Reserve continued slashing interest rates to 45-year lows of one per cent. With banks and other financial institutions increasingly greedy for profits, and with a financial regulator asleep at the wheel, it was a perfect storm for a financial crisis.

The catalysts for the global financial crisis were falling US house prices and a rising number of borrowers unable to repay their loans. In the summer of 2007, the US subprime market collapsed and the crisis quickly spread to other world economies through a combination of direct exposures to subprime assets and the gradual loss of confidence across the entire global financial market. By October 2008, the crisis had led to the erosion of almost US$10 trillion in market capitalization from global equity markets with more than 30 per cent of new businesses collapsing. Most of the current economic forecasts predict the economic and social damage of COVID-19 will exceed the damage done by the GFC.

So how does business survive during these crises and how is it that some companies manage to profit from crises like these? The Apple Corporation provides insight into what creative and innovative companies do. Apple's approach to a crisis is to focus on its business and closely monitor and assess the changing economic environment. Apple's survival plan to get through the COVID-19 crisis is both complex and incredibly simple: stay focused, keep investing, stay optimistic, and take care. Apple CEO, Tim Cook, explained, "That's going to mean more investment in research and development as the company strives to find answers to the new questions we face post-pandemic."

Cook's approach mirrors much of what the company did when Steve Jobs was CEO during the GFC, and the crisis before that when the dot-com bubble burst in 2001. Jobs unveiled the iPhone on January 9, 2007, but it didn't go on sale until June 29 – right at the beginning of the GFC. That six-month gap was pure Jobs genius. During that period, Apple continued to refine its product and formed global partnerships with telco carriers. In a little over a year, that first iPhone sold over six million units and launched the smartphone revolution – and it all happened during a global financial crisis. As of 2020, Apple has sold more than 2.2 billion iPhones worldwide. This was all achievable because of Jobs' creativity, vision, and willingness to take risks.

Creativity bestows upon creators the agility to make the most of any situation. Creative thinking has the potential to turn bad into good, misfortune into fortune, and hate into love. It's a way of living that provides for rewards for everything you do. And this reward provides the motivation to continue to support the development of creative habits.

You Want to Change? You Can't Handle the Change!

One of the most difficult of all life's choices is the decision to change. We must overcome the inertia of comfortability. We must stop acting habitually and making only those choices that are reinforced through our ongoing acceptance of maintaining the status quo. With the corona event, we have a wake-up call that highlights the fact that there are choices we can make about how we can live our lives and what we want our next normal to look like.

First, we need to learn to de-school ourselves from our societal classroom, but to do so, we must break some deep-seated habits that direct you along this path of routine and social conformity.

Many people may wish, aspire, or even hope for a better life, but unfortunately most are not prepared to embrace the intra-personal change required for betterment. There are some who forever complain about change and aren't prepared to accept change or to concede that change will bestow any benefit on themselves or others. Then there are others who genuinely appear to want to change but don't have the passion or drive to motivate them to instigate the change they desire. And still there are others who make the decision to change but lack the willpower to keep the dream alive. If an individual or organization isn't sufficiently motivated to change the way they approach things, then they certainly will never be motivated to create.

There's an old joke that goes something like: How many psychologists does it take to change a lightbulb? Answer: Just the one, but the lightbulb has got to *want* to change. If you want to change for the better, you have first got to want to change.

There have been many occasions when someone I first meet discovers I was a professional pilot and comment along the lines: "I've always wanted to be a pilot." This makes me think: "Am I missing something here? Anyone can learn to fly a plane, so what's the problem?" What I usually suggest is a reputable local flying school or the name of a good flying instructor. But then the story changes. "Actually, I'm really afraid of heights," or perhaps, "Oh I'm far too old for that now."

On face value, these are seemingly rational responses, but are, in fact, incorrect. And even worse, they're a monumental cop out. These people are simply not sufficiently motivated to *really* want to change. A close friend of mine, Johnny McGuirk, has been a commercial pilot for the past 30 years, flying everything from blimps to Lear Jets, and he's petrified of heights. Another pilot-student friend of mine started flying at the age of 72 when he "finally got some spare time," he told me. These excuses are just that – reasons we convince ourselves of why we can't change.

Albert Einstein once said, "I have no special talents – I am only passionately curious." Being motivated by passion is by far the most effective catalyst to initiate change.

And of course, you are never too old or young to become passionate about anything.

An Australian friend of mine, who I will call Will, always wanted to be an airline pilot but family and work commitments always took priority. By the time Will turned 50, he had attained a Commercial Pilots' License by passing all the examinations and flying on the weekends. Will knew that the local airlines, quite incongruous with anti-discrimination legislation, only recruited more junior pilots, mainly because younger recruits provide a greater return on investment toward the cost of airline-pilot training. But all this changed when Richard Branson established Virgin Blue Airlines in Australia. The company threw traditional airline recruitment practices out the window, and when they named Australian businessman, Brett Godfrey, as its first CEO, his creative approach to hiring mirrored that of Branson.

Will saw this change in the airline industry as an opportunity. He signed up for a $50,000 training program with Boeing, took his long service leave, and spent the next five weeks in the US earning a type rating on a Boeing 737. The largest aircraft he had previously flown was a six-seater, twin-engine propeller-powered plane.

So, when Godfrey caught wind of Will's initiative and motivation, he was so impressed that he offered Will a place on the next pilot intake. The last I heard was that Will had recently earned his captaincy and had accumulated some 8,000 hours as an airline pilot. And by all accounts, he's loved every second of it. The only thing separating Will from those other wannabe pilots I meet is *passion*.

Similarly, when Mick Jagger was just 17, he informed his parents he was going to pursue a career as a musician. His parents desperately pleaded with him to try and find a real job. Half a century later, at the tender age of 70-something, Mick is still doing what he loves. Mick and The Rolling Stones have sold over 250 million albums, performed at over 2,000 stadium-filled concerts, and amassed an incredible US$15bn in sales revenue. During their 50th anniversary tour in the US alone, the band played before two million fans at over 100 sold-out venues with ticket sales in excess of US$1bn. They don't need the money or fame; they just love what they do. And all because they followed their passion. People, even some of the most influential people in your life like your family and loved ones, might tell you to get a real job, but if you choose to follow your true passions, then that's more of a real job than anything else could ever be.

So how does passion and creativity relate? To begin, you are far more likely to be creative in an area that you truly enjoy and love, rather than pursuing a career or undertaking for which you have no real desire or interest. Most behavioral psychologists agree that when someone is passionate and in a good mood, happy in what they are doing, more trusting of their intuition, then they are far more likely to be creative. Mick Jagger, in teaming up with guitarist Keith Richards, became a creative song-writing powerhouse and did so by being passionate about what they do.

A similar rush of passion happened to me during my corona event in Vanuatu when I started playing around with my electric keyboard. I remember one night staying up until dawn writing a song that just *had* to be written. I hadn't had so much fun in creating music since the days of my university rock 'n roll band. Passion is an incredibly motivating force. Though you may be able to derive some degree of satisfaction from any vocation or endeavor, most creative people choose to follow the path of their passions and find great satisfaction in their accomplishments.

People who think creatively tend to be intrinsically motivated, meaning that they're motivated to act from some internal desire, rather than a need for external reward or recognition. The members of The Rolling Stones certainly weren't motivated by money or fame when they embarked upon their 50th anniversary tour. And my friends Will and Johnny sure weren't either. Many psychologists believe that creative people find the intrinsic motivation of challenging activities energizing, and research suggests that simply thinking of intrinsic reasons to perform an activity may be enough to ignite the creative flame.

A passion for change need not extend to major life-changing events such as seeking a new career, getting married, or moving to the other side of the world. Practicing creators become passionately involved in anything from problem solving to wanting a new car or learning to play the piano. Passion can overcome your resistance to change. Genuine passion will always overcome fear – fear of failure, fear of losing, and of course, fear of changing. As with love, when we are truly passionate about something, it's almost as if we're in another world – a world less demanding and unconstrained by the inhibitions that society imposes upon us.

One of my all-time favorite musicians was John Lennon. As a child growing up in England, I remember watching on black-and-white TV, The Beatles' first televised performance of their new hit single, "She Loves You." I vividly recall watching the broadcast at the Great Fosters Hotel on BBC's *Sunday Night at the London Palladium*. Everything about them was different: their haircuts, their clothes, their stage antics, but above all, their unique style of music. I also remember many 'old' people at the time, including my parents, saying words to the effect: "They won't last – people won't even remember The Beatles in a few years' time." Six months after this performance, The Beatles had all top five singles on the US Billboard chart. After over half a century, The Beatles are still considered one of the, if not the, most influential bands of all time. And it all happened because they were different and intensely passionate about what they did.

John Lennon once said:

> *"There are two basic motivating forces: fear and love. When we are afraid, we pull back from life. When we are in love, we open to all that life has to offer with passion, excitement, and acceptance. We need to learn to love ourselves first, in all our glory and our imperfections. If we cannot love ourselves, we cannot fully open to our ability to love others or our potential to create. Evolution and all hopes for a better world rest in the fearlessness and open-hearted vision of people who embrace life."*

Apple founder, Steve Jobs, saw the world in a similar light: "You have to be burning with an idea, or a problem, or a wrong that you want to right. If you're not passionate enough from the start, you'll never stick it out."

This is where technology and innovation enter the creative equation. Innovation is the practice of making changes to things that are already established, whereas creativity enhances and improves upon existing concepts, practices, or processes. In other words, innovation is the process of applied creativity – doing something new that makes life better. Like creativity, an innovative mindset becomes ingrained through building the habit of thinking in certain ways and is nurtured in an environment conducive to creative thinking and rewarded through intrinsic gratification.

Success for companies in our post-COVID-19 world seems now dependent upon the promotion of creativity and innovation to provide the agility to seize the opportunities that our changed environment presents. As we previously saw, Steve Jobs introduced the iPhone during a devastating global financial crisis, and in the same year, Apple recorded a record profit. The culture of creativity and innovation allowed Apple to succeed despite the economic conditions of the time.

Finding your passion in life defines the starting line from which your race to a creative lifestyle begins. As with any race there must be a goal. Your race, your challenge, your mission, and your life – it's all up to you to start by defining what your goal is and what values in life are important to you. 20-20 Thinking is the process by which you can turn your goal into reality. But defining precisely what your goal is usually takes considerable time and effort and is part of the thought process. Your 20-20 Thinking begins with your *concept*; this is, the "C" in the C-R-E-A-T-E process. Just like Steve Jobs suggests, passion must be our driving motivator to develop our concept and see it through to its realization.

Armed with passion and a goal, let's now consider the argument for change. Mahatma Gandhi once said, "You must be the change you wish to see in the world." Grow in your own particular way. Nobody can go back and start a new beginning, but everyone can start and make a new ending. So, if you're in a rut and what you're doing is not your passion, what do you have to lose through embracing change? After all the only difference between a rut and a grave are the dimensions. We have all overcome obstacles in the past, so now is the time to embrace opportunities that can change your life. Your life will not get better by chance alone, it will only get better through change. You should remind yourself on a daily basis: only I can change my life. No one else can do that.

The fundamental requirement of making a passionate commitment to individual change is still only our starting point. It's the start of our six-step 20-20 Thinking journey. Along our path of creative thinking we must maintain our genuine and unequivocal desire to change, accompanied with our passion to commit. To assist us with our transition to a new way of thinking, and one that supports a creative mindset, we must better understand what's holding us back to making the type of change we want to make. Doing this will provide us with the rationale and reason in support of change and provide us with positive reinforcement that change is both desirable and necessary for us to attain goals, whether they are personal or professional.

The Risky Business of Playing it Safe

The inertia of maintaining the status quo is the hallmark of any society and is fundamentally the result of frozen thinking. As we saw earlier, Maslow's hierarchy of human needs suggests that one of our most basic and primitive human instincts is being and wanting to be part of a society. For Maslow; "It's not something we necessarily desire, it's something we necessarily are." After all, we are human beings and society is all about being human. Playing it safe in society translates to doing what society expects you to do to maintain social conformity. But playing it safe may prove to be the least safe option personally or professionally. From a corporate perspective, there can be no better example of the risks associated with playing it safe than to examine the near-death experience of the world's most profitable company.

The roots of International Business Machines, or IBM, date back to the 1880s. Nicknamed 'Big Blue', IBM is a multinational computer technology and IT consulting corporation headquartered in Armonk, New York. In the second half of the 20th century, IBM was known as one of the world's largest computer companies and systems integrators. In the 1960s and '70s, IBM controlled 70 per cent of the market for mainframe computers worldwide, and by the 1980s, it was the most profitable company in the world.

During the '80s, the phrase "no one ever got fired for buying IBM" became popular. The statement provided a fantastic marketing message and IBM loved it. The idea was that IBM was so well known, trusted, and reliable that it was the safest choice for any technology decision-maker. As long as you chose IBM, you were not going to get in trouble, no matter how costly or ineffective the resulting solution turned out to be.

But it's what is implied by the message that is of more concern. The phrase is an excellent example of understanding loss aversion or defensive decision making. The promotion of fear, uncertainty, and doubt (or FUD) is often used as a disinformation tactic in sales, marketing, politics, talkback radio, public relations, religious organizations, and propaganda. As a strategy, the goal is to disseminate negative, dubious, or even false information to influence public perception and is a manifestation of the appeal to fear. In essence, it accentuates the risks associated with change.

Fear of loss or failure is a far more powerful influencer of our behavior than the desire for gain, reward, or to succeed. This applies to corporate strategies and decisions that affect our everyday personal lives. In a commercial context, if a company can harness fear, they can charge a premium on both products and services. As the extract from John Lennon mentioned, fear is a very powerful motivating force. Fear of the unknown and fear of the different are the same pressures and indoctrinations that are continually opposing creative thought. We cannot escape these influences while remaining part of them. They are societal influences and we are all part of society.

To devise a creative solution to a problem, we first must realize that *there is* a problem. To realize there is a problem, we first must escape the surrounds and venture to a place where the problem is yet to manifest.

In the 1980s, IBM didn't see that they had a problem. As a century-old business, and at the time the world's most profitable company, why wouldn't you keep doing things the way you always had? However, by the end of the decade, the company was in decline and at the beginning of the '90s, it was losing money big time. Between 1991 and 1993, IBM had cumulated losses of US$16 billion, with a staggering US$8.1 billion loss in 1992 alone. This was the largest single-year corporate loss in US history. IBM's near demise in the early '90s was due to a toxic mix of missed market trends, losing touch with its customers, but above all, it had developed a corporate culture incapable of change.

How did Big Blue break free from its predicament? IBM began by recognizing its strengths and its weaknesses, being candid about the fact that it had problems, but most importantly, identifying why it was having them. In short, IBM realized that in the changed commercial environment of increased competition and rapidly advancing technologies, it could no longer rest on its laurels. IBM needed to change its culture, and that could only happen from the top.

The next part of the IBM story is equally legendary. The IBM board hired Lou Gerstner as its new CEO, someone from outside the tech industry, and an IBM outlier. For the first time in 80 years, Big Blue had recruited a leader from beyond its ranks. Gerstner was a dynamic, innovative, and creative senior executive from American Express. Many anticipated Gerstner would break-up the company for sale. While briefly entertaining this thought, Gerstner concluded IBM was more valuable as one business, provided it could overcome what is sometimes termed "active inertia." This is when a company's set of assumptions about its core business inhibits new ways of thinking, and this inertia, or resistance to change, is perpetuated through frozen thinking. IBM had to change its way of thinking about itself and everything around it so that it could capitalize on the opportunities provided by change.

Gerstner and his senior executives set about establishing a sense of urgency to fix IBM's problems. The major focus was to re-establish the IBM brand. The company's marketing during its economic downturn was chaotic, presenting many different, and sometimes contradictory, messages to the marketplace. This brand confusion was largely attributable to the company having retained 70 different advertising agencies. Within a year, Gerstner consolidating all its marketing and advertising strategies within the one agency and eliminated this chaos. The result was a coherent, cohesive, and consistent message to the marketplace, and most important – to its employees. In establishing the One IBM philosophy, Gerstner had set a vision for the company as a global information business. IBM was then well positioned to capitalize on new opportunities that had arisen through technological developments, in particular, the arrival of the internet.

The IBM experience highlights that for organizations to succeed in our volatile and competitive post-COVID-19 environment, creativity needs to be their primary focus. Survival will rest on creative individuals driving creative organizations. These individuals and organizations may not be able to predict what the next normal will look like, but they will be able to see what's more important: they will be able to make the most of the world around them. They will have a vision, with creative ideas that can conceptualize what's required to succeed and prosper within their contemporary, but rapidly changing environment. The CEOs, and the organizations they lead, are agile, adaptive, and responsive, and all because of the organizational culture they've created. It requires a culture that promotes and rewards ingenuity and innovation. In short, these organizations have created a culture of creativity.

The IBM story has a happy ending. Although the traditional IBM approach of playing it safe and doing things the way they'd always done them had served the tech giant well for over a century, such an approach in today's rapidly changing commercial environment is akin to corporate suicide. Modern society has become extremely competitive, but at the same time, increasingly complex and far more strictly regulated.

IBM managed to acknowledge and address its problems just in time. However, Blackberry, MySpace, Yahoo, Dell Computers, Eastman Kodak, Encyclopedia Britannica, Pan Am, and countless more who were less responsive to change have paid the ultimate corporate price. In the rapidly changing COVID-19 world, agility derived from our resolve to innovate is the only effective force for individuals and corporations to attain success. And the only way to sustain long-term innovation and growth is through creativity – as a personal trait of an individual or as the culture within an organization.

To foster profitable growth as we move to our next normal, established businesses must be able to pursue new opportunities that are provided through the COVID-19 pandemic. If a business' core products or service offerings are being carried in the river of commercialization, that business must avoid the current and get upstream to where new opportunities arise. Today, very few corporations are afforded the protection provided by yesterday's sheltered industries. Competition is fierce across every commercial sector.

Consider the airline industry. The effects of COVID-19-related border closures and stay-at-home orders around the world have had devastating effects on international and domestic travel. On the other side of the pandemic and in the years to come, airlines and travel will emerge as an entirely new industry as those who do survive attempt to recover their massive losses. But revolutionary changes have happened before in the aviation sector. The proliferation of low-cost carriers like EasyJet, JetBlue, Ryanair, and AirAsia have completely changed the way we travel by air. Similarly, companies like Uber and Lyft have completely revolutionized the way we move about cities. And look no further than Airbnb and the hospitality sector to see how swiftly new ideas can arise and change the long-established course of the mighty waterways of industries.

Companies like Uber, Airbnb, and AirAsia highlight the importance of creativity and how seeing a different way of doing things in our rapidly changing world may provide the winning formula for success. There are many reasons to explain why creativity is a necessary attribute. Creativity is the one thing that cannot be outsourced. Creativity can provide for a more efficient use of existing resources. For businesses, creativity may be the difference between success and failure. Although businesses may have traditionally hired individuals based on their qualifications and experience, in our post-pandemic world, progressive organizations will promote those that have the ability to think creatively. In business and in personal endeavors, creativity will become the currency of accomplishment.

IBM's story demonstrated the risky business of playing it safe in the world of commerce, but the same can be applied to our everyday lives. The play-it-safe fallacy applies equally to our personal lives but with the added potential of a disastrous outcome that many of us may take to our graves.

In a 1994 study published in the *Journal of Personality and Social Psychology*, researchers found that the biggest regrets people held tended to involve things they had failed to do in their lives, as opposed to, say, the silly actions they took. The researchers suggested that in the short-term, actions were more likely to cause more pain, but in the long run, people regretted their inactions more. Recent studies conducted by Shai Davidai and Thomas Gilovich have looked deeper into the psychology of regret and show that the most enduring regrets that people have stem from "discrepancies between their actual and ideal selves [rather] than their actual and ought selves." This is because we're quicker to deal with our failures of action than we are the failures to live up to our dreams, passions, and ambitions. The researchers state, "as a consequence, ideal-related regrets are more likely to remain unresolved, leaving people more likely to regret not being all they could have been more than all they should have been."

It's sad that so many amongst us are living unhappy lives and yet not prepared to take the initiative to change their predicament. They seem conditioned to a life of security, conformity, and preservation. They have assumed a play-it-safe mentality. Although these traits appear to give them peace of mind, in reality, nothing could be further from the truth. They simply perpetuate their personal status quo. They have lost, or never had in the first place, a dream to imagine a better life. As per the previous reflections of the late Douglas Adams: "If you don't change your beliefs, your life will be like this forever. Is that good news?"

The major impediment to creativity in most of us is that we're all conditioned in the way we think. Yet as we've seen throughout this chapter, this conditioning is the by-product of our upbringing, our family, education, religion, our workplace, and other societal influences. Society as we know it couldn't function if this were not the case. Society is society because it conditions us and requires conformity. We are social if we conform, and society is quick to label us outcasts if we don't. As Maslow maintained, being and wanting to be part of society is one of our most basic and primitive human instincts.

The coronavirus pandemic is an opportunity to reinvent ourselves and the organizations we work for by looking at life and the world differently. Your life will not get better by chance alone, it will only get better through change. You should remind yourself on a daily basis – only I can change my life. No one else can do that for you. Now, let's get started!

Learnings from Chapter 1:
You need to become more comfortable with change and make change your friend. But the change you need must come from within. Then you can start to see and realize the opportunities that are presented through a changed environment.

Now go to **Chapter 6 – Habits** and relate the above learnings to the following habits:
- Habit #1 Do you challenge the status quo?
- Habit #2 Are you curious about why things are the way they are?

2

HOW TO SEE THE WORLD DIFFERENTLY

"Reality is merely an illusion, albeit a very persistent one."

Albert Einstein

In the previous chapter we saw that opportunity often arises amid a world of rapid change. Our ability to adapt to new environments determines the likelihood of making the most of a situation and seizing the opportunities we're missing. Even during times of crises – as we've experienced with the COVID-19 pandemic – opportunities abound, it's just that most of us are wired in such a way that we can't see them. Learning to think differently enables us to start seeing the world from a different perspective.

For us to see the world differently, we need to focus on changing the way we think. As we saw in Chapter 1, our corona dilemma has required us to make a choice between returning to our normal world or choosing to start doing things differently. If we want to *create* our next normal that will support our re-assessed values in life, we must make the *right* decisions. This chapter is all about preparing our mind to start thinking differently and thinking creatively so we can start making those decisions.

In his book, *The Art of Creative Thinking*, author Rod Judkins wrote that, "Creativity is not about creating a painting, novel or house but creating *yourself*, creating a better future and taking the opportunities you are currently missing." To unlock the secrets of creativity, we need to gain a good understanding of the unique thought processes behind creative thinking. What is it about creative individuals that enables them to identify and make the most of opportunities? How are so many novel ideas so accessible to these people and yet totally inconceivable for the rest of us? To be creative in how we think does not require superior intelligence. Most of us are smart enough to think like these creative "geniuses," so what makes them capable of forming these connections that the rest of us do not?

When questioned about what makes him think the way he does, Tesla Motors co-founder, Elon Musk simply answered, "I guess I'm just wired that way." Neuroscientists now know that brain neurons that fire together, wire together. It *is* possible to get to work on our own brain wiring, but first we need to explore the workings of the thought processes that Elon and other practicing creatives like him undertake in their everyday life. We need to understand the psychology of how we think and how we perceive things.

To effectively participate in our changed post COVID-19 environment, we need to change the way we think. And for most of us this will require a paradigm shift.

Pardon My Paradigm

In social science, the term "paradigm" is used to describe the set of values that affect the way an individual perceives the world. Essentially, our paradigms determine the way we connect with the world. Our paradigms are a culmination of input that's derived from three sources:

1. What you *know* (everything you have learned)
2. What you have *experienced* (everything that has happened to you)
3. What you *believe* (your imaginings, mental images, or values)

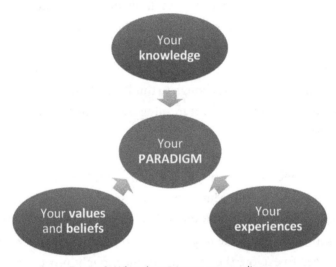

Figure 3: What determines your paradigm

With the onset of COVID-19, every one of us experienced the effects of the pandemic – social distancing, self-isolating, and staying at home. For those who experienced a corona event, this also resulted in the reassessing of our values and beliefs and those things in life that really matter. Whether these new values become part of who we are going forward is all dependent upon whether or not these values become *core* values.

I'm sure we've all at some time made, or at least contemplated, a New

Year's resolution. Let's assume that you've made a resolution to exercise three times a week. So now what happens? You religiously go to the gym three times a week up until, say, mid-February when things start getting a bit frantic at work, then you slip down to two days a week, and by March it's every other week, and so on. I think you get the picture.

What's happened here is that even with the best intentions, you really tried to keep up your routine, but you failed. Back on New Year's Eve, you genuinely wanted to change your personal value of putting a higher priority on staying healthier but this didn't pan out because more pressing and immediate needs like work commitments, driving kids to music lessons and sporting venues, and doing household chores were competing with your resolution. What happened is that your newly re-assessed value of staying healthier turned out to be nothing more than a superficial, short-lived aspiration. There was no change to your core values and hence no paradigm shift.

Busy life, busy schedules, competing priorities. It's easy to deduce that the things we actually do in life simply comes down to doing the things that we feel we *really* have to do. It's the way we prioritize our choices that determines those things that get done and those that don't; irrespective of whether they're desirable things or the things you know you just have to get done.

Now let's return to that New Year's resolution and change the scenario and suppose you've been selected to compete in the national handball selection trials commencing in July for the Olympic Games in the following year. It has been your number one goal since you were in junior high school to one day represent your country in handball. Your coach has set you a demanding training schedule, but you *really* want to do more. You decide upon a New Year's resolution to exercise more and you know this resolution will be resolved.

The same applies to my friend, Will, in Chapter 1 who, at the age of 50, decided to become a pilot. He, too, had work and life commitments that would always take priority over achieving his dream. It wasn't until he made a conscious decision to shift his paradigms that he was able to turn that dream into a reality.

If you have resolved your corona dilemma in favor of really wanting to change your ways to ensure your reassessed values will be part of your next normal, then this will become a core value. To change your core values and to make a paradigm shift, you need to support your new way of seeing the world with habits that promote these new values. Throughout this book we learn what these habits are and how to develop them, but before we can do that, we need to better understand how our paradigms function.

Your paradigm influences the way you perceive the world, and in turn, how you respond to your perceptions. For instance, when Albert Einstein formulated his theory of general relativity, it revolutionized the scientific world because it had previously perceived the world based on the Newtonian model of physics. Scientists had to undergo a paradigm shift to view their new world from a relativity paradigm. Correct or incorrect, your paradigms are the source of your values, attitudes, behaviors, and ultimately, your relationship with others. To better understand the nature of our paradigms, it may be helpful to consider how our reasoning or cognitive processes operate. In his search for a new paradigm, British philosophy guru, Will Pye believes that it all comes down to *how* we perceive.

We typically imagine that the act of perception involves something *out there* to perceive and something *in here* perceiving, the one separate from the other. Such an assumption is so widely held as to be regarded as common sense, obvious, and beyond question. Unexamined experience supports this assumption – it certainly seems like there is a chair over there and me perceiving it here. It seems like there is my life out there and my description of it apart from it. Yet if we look more closely, we discover the experience of there being an inner and outer is a misperception. This quandary draws parallels with the concept of dualism and the mind-body problem. This question arises when mind and body are considered as distinct, based on the premise that the mind and the body are fundamentally different in nature. Pye says this division is a useful ploy that allows the wonderful experience of being human.

According to Pye, when we see the partiality of this assumption, when we see that there is just one thing or no-thing and that there is no world separate from the perceiving or, to put it another way, there is no perceiving separate from the world, we discover an astonishing new reality – we see that the world is dreamt into being in each moment. Your perception is your reality. You see the world not as it is but as you are.

To better explain let's consider a real-life example. To perceive that it is raining, it must be true that it is raining. And should we seek to attain objective evidence to confirm our perception then this is readily available by stepping outside and getting drenched. We can also perceive the world to be a certain way and yet be mistaken. This we can call, "perceiving as," or as is more common, "seeing as" or "hearing as." For instance, what is this a picture of?

Perhaps you see a duck. I can, however, alter the character of your visual experience by changing the beliefs that you have about this picture. Think RABBIT looking upward. The picture now looks different to you even though you're seeing the same configuration of a black line and a dot on a white background. Originally, you saw the drawing as a duck; now you see it as a rabbit.

But what about real life experiences? How can a paradigm-changing experience occur at a personal level? In his international bestselling book, *Seven Habits of Highly Effective People*, Dr Stephen R. Covey provides the following example involving an event that instantly changed his personal paradigm.

> *"People were sitting quietly – some reading newspapers, some lost in thought, some resting with their eyes closed. It was a calm, peaceful scene. Then suddenly, a man and his children entered the subway car. The children were so loud and rambunctious that instantly the whole climate changed. The man sat down next to me and closed his eyes, apparently oblivious to the situation. The children were yelling back and forth, throwing things, even grabbing people's papers. It was very disturbing. And yet, the man sitting next to me did nothing. It was difficult not to feel irritated. I could not believe that he could be so insensitive as to let his children run wild like that and do nothing about it, taking no responsibility at all.*
>
> *It was easy to see that everyone else on the subway felt irritated, too. So finally, with what I felt like was unusual patience and restraint, I turned to him and said:*
>
> *"Sir, your children are really disturbing a lot of people. I wonder if you couldn't control them a little more?"*

The man lifted his gaze as if to come to a conscious-
ness of the situation for the first time and said softly;

"Oh, you're right. I guess I should do something
about it. We just came from the hospital where their
mother died about an hour ago. I don't know what
to think, and I guess they don't know how to handle
it either."

Can you imagine what I felt at that moment? My
paradigm shifted. Suddenly I saw things differently,
and because I saw differently, I thought differently,
I felt differently, I behaved differently. My irritation
vanished. I didn't have to worry about controlling
my attitude or my behavior; my heart was filled with
the man's pain. Feelings of sympathy and compas-
sion flowed freely.

"Your wife just died? Oh I'm so sorry! Can you tell
me about it? What can I do to help?"

Everything changed in an instant."

The situation regarding organizations undergoing radical change as a result of an event or changed environment is much the same as it is for individuals. The main difference being that change to the core values of an organization or corporation is referred to as *cultural change* rather than a paradigm shift. All large organizations develop their own culture. A corporate culture refers to the shared values (what is important) and beliefs (how things work) that interact with an organization's structure and control systems to produce behavioral norms (the way we do things around here). In other words, a corporate culture is akin to an individual's paradigm in that it determines how a company will respond to the world around it.

To give you a commercial example of how an organization can change its core values, I need look no further than to the aviation industry. Aviation safety is an extremely emotive topic. And rightly so. Whenever the safety and wellbeing of humans is concerned, there is, and always should be, a high degree of public interest. The kind of scrutiny and monitoring of aviation safety attracts, especially in the media, is to a certain extent disproportion to the level of risk it poses to the community. Whether this level of scrutiny is warranted is a separate issue, but the fact remains that aviation safety is always prominent in the public eye and never far from the mind of even the most seasoned frequent flier.

Provided an airline has a healthy safety culture, then their ability to effectively transition to a new environment should be relatively straight forward. In some instances, however, deep-rooted cultural attitudes, those which are not conducive or consistent with safety practices, may obstruct or subvert attempts at change. Due to the unprecedented sanctions imposed under COVID-19 measures, especially with the closure of national boarders, the entire global airline sector is on life support as it struggles to survive. It concerns me greatly whether those airlines that survive the coronavirus pandemic will maintain the requisite levels of financing to ensure air travel remains safe. For this to happen, airline executives will need to support such expenditure and governments will need to remain vigilant to ensure that they do. There's a saying in the industry that "a safe airline is a profitable airline." And it further concerns me that as we move toward our next normal the re-emerging airline sector bears all the hallmarks of another time when the industry faced such an extraordinary and unprecedented change.

That time was October 24, 1978 when President Jimmy Carter signed the *Airline Deregulation Act* into law, marking the first time in the nation's history that *any* industry was deregulated. Under the new act, airlines were now free to determine their own fares and routes, an event that overnight transformed the industry and the entire passenger experience.

U.S. airline deregulation was a part of a greater global airline liberalization trend. Established airlines rushed to gain or preserve access to the most lucrative routes and a new breed of airlines quickly formed, becoming known as "no-frills airlines" (today they have the more palatable title of "low-cost carriers"). Unsurprisingly, fierce competition resulted and immediately drove fares down. Passengers flocked to airports in record numbers. Most of the incumbent carriers strongly opposed deregulation and insisted that the safety of airline passengers would be compromised. Their fears of a destabilized industry were well founded.

One of the new no-frills airlines was ValuJet. Operations commenced in 1993 with just two planes, and after a year of tremendous growth and the addition of 15 aircraft, the company listed on the stock exchange. ValuJet became the fastest airline to make a profit in the history of American aviation, earning $21 million in its first year of operations, and their shareholders loved it. But there was a trade-off. With aggressive cost cutting across all areas of the business, the airline's expansion relied on buying aging aircraft from around the world. The strategy left the company with a fleet that became the oldest in the United States, averaging 26 years. By way of comparison the average age of aircraft operated by full-service carriers in 2020 was less than 12 years.

Very quickly the airline developed a reputation for its poor attitude to safety and dangerous cost-cutting measures. Whatever work that could be contracted was farmed out to temporary employees and independent contractors. Industry stalwarts considered ValuJet's operations as "smoke and mirrors" often referring to it as a "virtual airline." The airline provided very little training to any of its employees, including their pilots, flight attendants, and aircraft engineers, and even required their pilots to pay for their own training. ValuJet were also skimping on staff payments, paying pilots *after* they completed flights and then at minimal salaries – about $43,000 plus bonuses for captains and around half that for co-pilots. The airline also subcontracted maintenance to several different companies who would then subcontract the work out to other companies. Whenever mechanics caused delays, ValuJet would cut the pay of the mechanics working on the plane. In just three years, the fleet had expanded from two planes to 52. In aviation speak, ValuJet was an accident waiting to happen.

And so, it did.

On May 11, 1996, after an hour-long mechanical delay, ValuJet Airlines Flight 592 took off from Miami International Airport just after 2 pm. Due to neglectful oversight, Flight 592 was illegally carrying 144 oxygen generators that were past their expiration dates and weren't properly stowed. Minutes after take-off, the generators began emitting oxygen, which, prodded by the heat in the cargo bay, soon caught fire. Just six minutes out of Miami, while climbing northwest through 11,000 feet, co-pilot Richard Hazen radioed air traffic control; "Ah, five-ninety-two needs an immediate return to Miami." In the deliberate calm of pilot talk this was strong language. The time was 32 seconds after 2:10 pm and it was a beautiful clear spring afternoon. Something had gone drastically wrong with the airplane. At 2:23 pm, the plane crashed into the Everglades, killing all 110 people onboard. Investigators later calculated that the airplane rolled to a 60-degree left bank and dove 6,400 feet in just 32 seconds. The airplane's speed at the time of impact was almost 500 miles an hour.

After the accident, and during a three-month FAA suspension, the board of directors realized that the only way the company had any chance of survival was by transforming the culture of the airline. It resumed flying with 15 of its newest jets, and in November 1996, announced Joseph Corr, a former and highly respected CEO of Continental Airlines, as the airline's CEO and President. Having lost over $55 million since the crash, Corr had a big job on his hands. His immediate focus went toward changing the most essential core value for *any* airline, namely developing a positive and genuine commitment to safety. A year later, Corr acquired the smaller AirTran Airways and dropped the name ValuJet and the transformation was complete.

In a 2010 article in the *New York Times*, AirTran was described as "one of the most unlikely success stories in the airline industry." In every year since the crash, the airline received the industry's highest and most prestigious safety award – the FAA's Diamond Award of Excellence. I recall back in 2001 when I was in LA undergoing pilot conversion training on the new Boeing 717 – the same aircraft type that AirTran had acquired – I met a bunch of AirTran trainee pilots. Within minutes of talking to these guys you could sense a real commitment to safety just in the way they spoke about the company, their training and their aspirations for the future with the company. The airline returned to profitability within a year of Corr taking over as CEO and became one of the most respected airlines within the industry.

Not all stories about airlines after major accidents ends up this way. Four days before Christmas in 1988, Pan Am Flight 103 exploded over Lockerbie, Scotland, killing all 259 people on board and 11 on the ground in the small Scottish town. This was the beginning of the end for Pan Am which was once America's largest international airline. After over 60 years of operations, Pan Am eventually filed for bankruptcy in 1991. Then just two months after the ValuJet crash in July 1996, TWA Flight 800 took off from JFK Airport headed for Paris. Twelve minutes later, it exploded over the shores of Long Island, New York. None of the 230 people on board survived. TWA never fully recovered from the crash and ceased operations in 2001.

More recently on March 8, 2014, Malaysia Airlines flight MH370 disappeared from the radar on a scheduled flight from Kuala Lumpur to Beijing. All 227 passengers and 12 crew members disappeared. The aircraft reached cruising level about half an hour after departing and 10 minutes later the Captain was instructed to switch radio frequencies. He said "Goodnight, Malaysia Three Seven Zero". The aircraft then bizarrely deviated from the scheduled route and flew across Malaysia, Sumatra, and then into the Indian Ocean before it disappeared off the radar. Still nobody knows what happened. Four months later, Malaysia Airlines Flight 17 (MH17) was flying from Amsterdam to Kuala Lumpur when it was shot down by a Buk surface-to-air missile while flying over the warzone in eastern Ukraine. All 298 people on board were killed.

While the MH370 incident was not necessarily the direct consequence of deficiencies within the airline, the financial losses and adverse public perceptions following the tragic incident led to the company making decisions that put its crew and passengers in danger. International aviation regulators had warned airlines of the increased hazards associated with flying over Ukrainian airspace, and many operators decided to divert around this region. By diverting around the active warzone, airlines increased their operating costs but likewise increased the level of safety.

All these accidents exemplify the adage "If you think safety is expensive, try having an accident." Some airlines just can't change their core values quick enough to restore the flying public's confidence for them to survive. Just as we saw how difficult it is for individuals to change the core values required for a paradigm shift, so too is the difficulty for corporations to change their core values necessary for a cultural change.

But how do companies change their culture?

When AirTran's CEO Joseph Corr turned around the misfortunes of ValuJet he knew that the most important aspect about cultural change within an organization was that it never filters up. Change *must* be driven from the very top of an organization for it to be absorbed by every employee. For over 8,000 employees, aviation safety had become their individual responsibility. As with personal paradigms, corporate culture is an incredibly powerful force.

Now that we've considered the process for changing core values of individuals and corporations, what about changing the core values of society? At a societal level, the situation is much the same in relation to the values and beliefs people have and how, over time, they may vary between communities, cultural groups, and countries. Consider the diversity of values people may have in respect to, say, smoking in restaurants, spitting in the street, or wearing short skirts in public. Different values, different beliefs, different paradigms. New paradigms that develop in society are often related to advances in technology, and there's no better example of this than in the changed way we communicate as a society, both personally and in business, since the advent and proliferation of the internet, laptop computers, and smart phones.

Not all paradigm shifts are advantageous at either the individual or societal level. What we need to do is to continually challenge ourselves and ask the question "is my paradigm helping or hindering me?" As a personal example, I know that I'm quite opinionated when it comes to music. If it's not something I like first off, I tend to reject it entirely. Obviously, such an attitude is limiting and restricts my ability to gain an insight into something completely different to my own lived experience. Some people may have a similar attitude when it comes to classical music or opera or whether they think Monty Python sketches are brilliant or stupid or whether pineapple belongs on a pizza.

Whether they move us in a positive or negative direction, whether they're instantaneous or incremental, paradigm shifts take us from one way of seeing the world to another. And those shifts create powerful change. Our paradigms, correct or incorrect, are the sources of our attitudes and behaviors, and ultimately our relationships with others. All these new paradigms develop because of our ability to perceive the world differently.

We create the world that we perceive, not because there is no reality outside our heads, but because we select and edit the reality we see to conform to our beliefs about what sort of world we live in. We make up our own realities. As Albert Einstein reminds us, reality is merely an illusion, albeit a very persistent one. So we live in worlds of our own based on meanings we give to every event, thought, and moment. We all see the world through different lenses, and the lenses you choose is the world you perceive. The lenses tint or filter our world according to our paradigms, so if we can choose which lenses to use, we can choose how we see things. We don't see things as they are, we see them as *we* are. We can consider this as being our paradigm of reality.

Our task at hand and the underlying objective of 20-20 Thinking is to shape our paradigms to protect those values we have determined as being important following our corona event. So, unless your paradigm provides for something that you truly believe in, then your reality will never accept that concept, value, or belief. For instance, if you don't believe in ghosts, then very rarely will any event or situation, no matter how scary it may be, allow for you to accept ghosts into your reality. It's not a matter of "I'll believe it when I see it," but rather, "I'll see it when I believe it."

So now let's consider an example to see how *our* paradigm of reality applies to the world around us.

News flash! Another meaningless, senseless mass shooting at a high school. A student with a semi-automatic assault rifle has slain a dozen of his fellow students. The media and public are outraged and call for action. What is the solution? One TV interviewee insists that an immediate ban on the sale of this type of weapon is the only answer. The next interviewee is convinced the only solution lies in ensuring all schools and teachers are properly armed to defend themselves and protect their students against future attacks. In this scenario the facts are the same, but the reaction is worlds apart. In response to this scenario, each individual has a view based on their paradigm so they each perceive an entirely different world – *their* world.

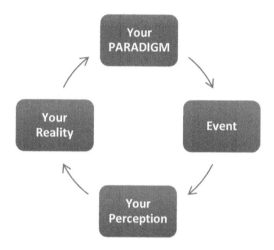

Figure 4: Paradigm of Reality - How we relate to the world

What makes for such divergent views is the paradigms that these two individuals bring to their respective perception and response to the same event. Each believes in their solution to the problem. Their individual paradigms provide an entirely different foundation upon which their respective perceptions of the situation are interpreted. This feeds their rationale for their response and solution.

In life we react and respond to things according to the reality we perceive, and this feeds back into our paradigm. And so, the cycle continues. All this is fine provided that our version of reality does not become at complete odds with the reality that's generally perceived by society. In some instances, society's assessment of reality prevails, even if it's inconsistent with a version of reality that can be proven by scientific discourse or objective evidence.

To introduce some scientific rigor into our discussion, it's worth considering what's commonly known as the McGurk Effect. In a paper published in 1976, cognitive researcher Harry McGurk described the perceptual phenomenon of the interaction between hearing and vision in speech perception. It's really worth viewing the BBC video documentary presentation now by Googling the "McGurk Effect". Do it now.

In the video, you'll see a close-up shot of the lips of a presenter repeatedly pronouncing the words "bah – bah – bah". Then the same spoken words are dubbed with the same presenter but this time with his lower lip touching the upper row of teeth to produce the expected "fah" sound. Amazingly these same repeated words "bah – bah – bah" are now acoustically perceived as "fah – fah – fah." Check out the video – it really is quite mind-blowing.

Source: www.bbc.co.uk

Figure 5: The McGurk Effect

So why do we hear something that's entirely different from what we *should* hear? The sensory illusion occurs when the auditory component of one sound is paired with the visual component of another sound, leading to the auditory perception, in this instance, of the original sound. The McGurk Effect is an illusion created in response to incongruent audio-visual stimuli. The visual information a person receives from seeing a person speak changes the way we hear the sound. In the scenario portrayed on the BBC video, the relevant component of our paradigm relates the seeing of a person speaking whose bottom lip is touching their upper teeth with the emission of the sound "fah" intrinsically associated with that scenario. Based upon our paradigm – what we have experienced, what we have learned, and what we believe – it's discordant to relate this visual experience with the emission of any sound other than a "fah." Moreover, because scientists believe that visual perception typically accounts for the majority of *how* we learn (seeing accounts for 83 per cent of how we learn, hearing 11 per cent, touching 3 per cent, smelling 2 per cent, and tasting 1 per cent), visual sensory input is the overwhelmingly dominant sense. Based on our paradigm, our brain unconsciously overrides and changes what we *hear* based on what we see. Even more amazing is the fact that even when we're aware of this illusion, we're still unable to override its effect. Cognitive biases are extremely powerful forces when it comes to how we perceive the world, or more precisely, *our* world.

Now let's consider a real-life scenario relating to sensory illusions. It's based upon my experiences as a flying instructor and considers the divergent perceptions of two pilots each flying in a small aircraft. One of the pilots is flying by sole reference to flight instruments while the other is flying visually, that is, looking for visual cues outside of the cockpit for orientation. Instrument-rated pilots are trained to fly an aircraft referencing only the aircraft's instruments – the flight attitude indicator, the altimeter, the vertical speed indicator and so on. These pilots are trained to condition themselves to *not* believe things are always the way they seem or feel. As we saw with the McGurk Effect, how we perceive sensory cues can distort reality.

Upon entering cloud, prior training instructs the instrument-rated pilot to continue flying straight (constant direction) and level (maintaining altitude) by sole reference to the aircraft's instruments. However, the VFR (visual flight rules) pilot, while searching for visual features, may believe they're continuing to fly straight and level when in fact they may, for example, be descending and turning at an ever-increasing angle of bank. This pilot is suffering from vertigo. As the pilot desperately searches for a non-existent visual horizon, he loses all sense of his situational awareness. Research (and unfortunately many fatal accidents) have proven that if a pilot who has been taught to fly only by visual references enters cloud, they will lose control of the aircraft in an average time of under three minutes – even if they are frantically trying to "fly on instruments."

In this situation the undisputed facts of a small aircraft entering cloud were the same for both pilots, but because of the two pilots' perception of reality being different, their view of the world is also different. These two pilots may well have similar attitudes and values in life, but because of a single variance of their knowledge and experiences, their entire view of the world is different. The latter pilot was prepared to bet their life on *their* version of reality. Perceptions, and the paradigms that shape them, are extremely powerful human forces.

As humans, practically everything we know is acquired through learning and experience. Much less of what we know, and how our paradigms are shaped, is determined by instinct or dictated by the genes we have inherited. So, if we wish to view the world through creative-tinted glasses, then we need to learn, or train ourselves, how to think creatively.

In certain instances, there are absolute truths concerning paradigms – although some may not be readily verifiable at the time. When Copernicus proclaimed the Earth rotates around the Sun, his assertion was rejected by the populous for more than a century as it conflicted with the then-accepted fact that the Earth was the center of the universe. Breaking with tradition and society's accepted way of thinking is not easy, even when the new paradigm concerns a provable fact. Society conditions us to feel more comfortable in accepting things as being the way we are told, even when it defies logic.

With the paradigm shift required for seeing the world in a different light with the intent of becoming more creative, there are no absolute truths. Paradigms that are difficult or impossible to prove or disprove are quite often the hardest to abandon. This is also why conspiracy theories persist.

Even when credible data and information is presented, the nature of conspiracy theories and their (sometimes warranted) mistrust of "official" findings means it's impossible to completely and irrefutably prove or disprove the theory. More generally, individuals and corporations have *faith* that the world is as they're told. People respond in a manner that society would expect them to and companies invest based on faith that the market trends are as they're told. But we should proceed with caution, as the renowned German philosopher Karl Jasper reminds us, "Faith is a leap beyond reason."

One of the core values you'll need to develop to undergo a paradigm shift to a new way of thinking is that of creativity. A creative paradigm provides you with a new mindset and one that you can apply to everything you do and enrich every aspect of your life. Creativity isn't just a switch that's switched on and off; it's a way of seeing, engaging with, and responding to the world around you. The creative are creative when cooking, playing golf (though some not particularly well), arranging timetables, developing marketing strategies, or watering the garden. By experiencing this paradigm shift, you change the way you think. This will change your world: for *your* world is as you perceive it. Remember, if you change the way you look at the world, the world you look at changes.

The world is not all factual, verifiable, and objective. But your world is *your* world and continues as such according to the paradigms you accept. This then determines how you perceive the world. Although perception may not be reality, in the mind of the perceiver, it is *their* reality. If you view the world through creative-tinted glasses, then this will be your new world.

If You Change the Way You Look at Things, the Things You Look at Change

This might all sound well and good, but how *do* you start to change the way you think? How do you rid yourself of almost a lifetime of thinking the way you've been taught to think? How do you begin to learn or relearn how to think differently? How can you learn to think creatively?

You may be thinking to yourself: But I am no Elon Musk; I am no Marie Curie; I am no Beyonce Knowles or Steve Jobs or Ada Lovelace. I am just one of the masses, a mere mortal in the company of greatness. They are different from me. Perhaps this is just who I am and how I was born – some creative and some, well, less creative.

Not true.

We are born neither creative nor non-creative. We are no more born creative than we are born polite, argumentative, or punctual. No one was ever born a racist but there are certainly many racists on our planet. We are what we learn or are taught to be. Fortunately, nowadays, there are far fewer racists in society because most contemporary societies promote inclusion and condone acts of racial vilification. Unfortunately, however, many societies don't support elements that promote creativity. In fact, they often do the opposite. Therefore, any change to a more creative mindset must come from within – that is, an *intra*-personal change – not change from societal or external influences.

What's required for us to understand the nature and essence of this topic is a journey into the realm of *metacognition* – thinking about what we're thinking about. To engage in metacognition, you must regularly ask yourself not "*what* am I learning?" but rather "*how* am I learning?" Ultimately, metacognition requires you to externalize mental events by engaging in what I call "thought excursions." This requires you to think in pictures and involves setting up a scene or image in your head and letting it run.

Consider the following problem that German psychologist Karl Dunker first posed in the 1940s. One morning a Buddhist monk sets out at sunrise to climb a path up the mountain to reach the temple at the summit. He arrives at the temple just before sunset. A few days later, he leaves the temple at sunrise to descend the mountain, traveling somewhat faster since it is downhill. The questions is: show that there is a spot along the path that the monk will occupy at precisely the same time of day on both trips.

Now if we start thinking about the problem in mathematical terms or in terms of rates and distances you will find that this makes finding a solution more difficult. If, however, we engage in thought excursions we can approach the problem by setting the scene in our mind. It's easy to visualize the path of the monk ascending the mountain, starting at dawn, and also his path descending the mountain, also starting at dawn. But think now of two monks to represent his two journeys, one walking up the trail and one walking down at the same time. The two monks must meet somewhere on the trail, therefore occupying the same spot on the trail at the same time of day. This type of visual thinking renders the solution as "intuitively" obvious.

How then are we going to change the way we think about problems and being more creative in how to solve them? Let's start by considering creativity not as a personality trait, but rather as a value or belief in life. It's something we can choose to do or be rather than something we are. As most of us have been raised to conform to societal expectations, social conditioning has suppressed or possibly even repressed our belief in our own creative capacities. Through the development of habits, we become locked into our non-creative ways of doing things.

If you have purchased or borrowed (or stolen!) this book, you're likely in search of a way of creating a new you. Ironically, your ability to create this new you is already within you, but for most of us, because we're too busy being someone else, our creative tendencies remain dormant. If, throughout life, we continue to do precisely as we're told, then we'll simply be replicating and reinforcing the status quo. Originality, which is a prerequisite for creative thinking, can never derive from pure replication. Creative people are prepared to be themselves. They make the most of their own experiences – for good and for bad. The advantage of being yourself is that you are an original, a one of a kind. This makes whatever you do original and sets you on the path of creative thinking.

Although we enter this world with potentially unlimited creativity, schools, workplaces, and societies beat that creativity out of us. We're feared into conformity from a very early age. In being immersed in society's brainwashing whirlpool it's little wonder there are so few creative geniuses around today. The greatest inhibitor of creative expression is the constant tsunami of societal indoctrination that dumps on us. Every. Single. Day.

Curiously, the word "society" derives from the Latin *socius* meaning "friend." Being social requires us to relate to society and the way society is organized. In so doing, we become a "friend" of society. If we don't relate to society in the way others do, then we're certainly not society's friend. We're considered social outcasts. Saying and doing things differently from others is a sure way of being branded "antisocial."

Society grooms us to worry or even fear saying the wrong thing, looking foolish, or having to take responsibility for a new idea, or heaven forbid, to fail. In fact, in my first year at university, I almost failed my science degree with a perfect four-out-of-four failures – and I wasn't even trying! (But man, did we have some great days at the White Horse Hotel!) Too often, institutions or the culture of an organization stifle their most valuable natural resource — the imagination and fresh ideas of its members or employees. In the case of institutions, particularly schools, this is usually a deliberate, stabilizing strategy, whereas for organizations it's more likely based on ignorance and a failure to understand and appreciate the value of promoting creative expression. "The only thing that interferes with my learning," Einstein once said, "is my education."

When my eldest son, Hugh, was just a child, I remember him looking up at the contrails of a high-flying jet streaking across a brilliant blue sky. He looked up at me, his eyes full of wonder, and said, "Dad, someone scratched the sky." This is a child's creative perception of something seen in the sky. British romantic poet, William Wordsworth, conveyed the sensation of walking in a field of daffodils in expressing the words, "I wandered lonely as a cloud." Creative perceptions and expressions of things in the sky may originate from the mind of a poet or a five-year-old child.

Allow me to let you in on a little secret. It is, in fact, the secret to eternal youth, the recipe for the elixir of life, the path to the fountain of youth. Regather your kindergarten crayons, throw away your high school education and societal indoctrinations, and start re-thinking the way you thought when you were a child, from the perspective and advantage of having amassed a treasure trove of life's experiences. This is how to start thinking differently. This is how to start thinking creatively. This is how you'll never get old.

Begin by taking a positive approach and fresh outlook to everything around you; not just the good things – everything. Start today. Now!

What I Choose Is My Choice

What an absolute pleasure is this thing we call life. For all its majesty, its terror, its vibrancy, and its poverty, life is the medium in which *all* exists. For good and for bad. And we, as humans, live the life we choose. Not necessarily the life that we *want*, but the life we *choose*.

Every day, every one of us has an infinite array of choices to make. Translating this in terms of choices – consciously or unconsciously – every one of us make around 30,000 decisions a day. Mostly, we aren't even cognizant of the fact that we have a choice because so much of what we do, we do habitually or instinctively. Recall from earlier that metacognition requires us to externalize mental events by engaging in thought excursions. We must challenge ourselves by considering not "what am I thinking?" but rather "how am I thinking?" Then the question becomes: "What are the choices I have, which choice am I going to accept, and what choice am I going to act upon?"

By way of a practical exercise to demonstrate the extent to which we're oblivious to the myriad of choices we're confronted with daily, consider the following:

The next time you're cleaning the kitchen after making breakfast, try this simple exercise in metacognition that will help to prime your brain for thought excursions. As you set about the task of putting things away in the cupboard or the fridge and cleaning up the mess, think about *how* you are thinking. To provide some framework, it may help if you think about how you might complete the task in the most efficient way possible. Look intensely at everything around you, including in your peripheral, and imagine how you can accomplish this mission most expeditiously. What things need to go in the cupboard and what's the optimal order for their return? How many items can I effectively and safely carry in one maneuver? What's the projected path around the kitchen to minimize travel time? And so on . . .

This may all sound a bit crazy, but you may discover that cleaning the kitchen will never be quite the same again. It's amazing how much better you can get with practice. Every time you do it, you'll uncover another element that will optimize the task and introduce a new dimension of creativity into your life. (From experience, you may also find it's also a good way to get your mind into gear on workdays.)

Let's consider a few more cerebral workouts, and perhaps somewhat less obscure exercises. Do you ever think or say to yourself:

"Which way am I going to commute to work today?"

"Will I acknowledge that new receptionist that I don't particularly like?"

"Am I going to have a croissant with my morning coffee today?"

Unlike lower order mammals, our behavior is generally less instinctive. As humans, we *do* have the superior intelligence to choose what we wish to do. Our ability to think and reason to a higher level is what sets us apart from other forms of life and every other living creature.

Our mind is the vehicle that enables us to navigate our lives and steer it in whichever direction we choose. But breaking with old habits is never easy nor is developing new ones – as we saw earlier with our attempt to start a new habit based on our New Year's Eve resolution to exercise three times a week. If we *really* want, we can choose to do things differently. As we saw when we changed the scenario and the motivation to achieve the goal was real, then the resolve of developing the habit of regular exercising was attainable. You *can* choose to do things differently. At the end of the day, it's up to you – and only you – to decide if you're going to even think about changing, and then deciding as to whether or not you will, in fact, change.

Recognizing and acknowledging the importance of change is the first step of any effective change management process. But the ability to change for the better requires more. Our ability to steer our lives in the *right* direction comes down to making the *right* choices. The right choice is to steer one's life or corporation in the direction that achieves desired outcomes.

We all make decisions over and over again in daily life. Many of those decisions are pretty straightforward—like choosing what you're going to watch on TV or what time you're going to have dinner. Others, like deciding to brush your teeth at night or grabbing a coffee at your favorite café on your way to work, are so much part of your routine that you don't even think of them as decisions because they've become habitual. During the coronavirus pandemic, even some easy decisions became hard because our daily routine has been derailed. But the choice of choosing the right decision is not always straightforward as many factors, both conscious and subconscious, affect our ability to make a rational decision.

Although we might think of ourselves as rational, the choices we make, especially those that are particularly important during a global pandemic, are not based purely on the best information we have. Experts in behavioral science and social psychology will tell us that we're all susceptible to biases that push and pull our brains in invisible ways. These are referred to as cognitive biases. Research shows that even the most minor of choices can be colored by our mood. Emotions have a profound effect on the process by which we make decisions. This is especially the case when dealing with incidental background emotions unrelated to the decision at hand that we're often unaware of how it influences our thinking. If we're feeling angry, depressed, sad, or excited, then these emotions can, in some way, affect the quality of the choices we make.

However, not all cognitive biases are based on our emotions. As we saw in Chapter 1, frozen thinking only allows us to consider information that confirms our pre-existing view of the world, so we maintain a certain confidence level of what we already believe.

To help assess whether or not you're making the right decision, I've devised a checklist covering what you should consider whenever you're making an important life choice. To illustrate the point, I return to the time when I experienced my corona event in Vanuatu and in particular my decision to resign from my long-held, secure position. When I look back now, I can clearly see why it was one of the best decisions I've ever made in my life, but at the time, I struggled long and hard to take the leap.

Step back and create your time-space oasis

Perhaps the biggest challenge a decision-maker faces is when to make the decision. Make it too slowly and events overtake you; too quickly and you risk acting rashly. However, researchers in cognitive psychologists have found that when people were asked about the most important decisions they've had to make, nearly all of them said that usually you've got more time than you realize to make the decision. You should therefore take time and make the space to reflect on your choices so that your emotions aren't driving your decision. Send a reply to that offending email *tomorrow*.

After a corona event, you need to make space to consider your values and priorities in life. This is what happened to me in Vanuatu. I knew I didn't have to make a decision overnight – in fact, I didn't even have to make a decision about leaving my job. But given time and space to reflect, I knew that I really *did* have to make a choice. And so, I did.

Other decisions are, of course, more time-sensitive, so setting aside time to assess the full range of options and when those deadlines are will similarly help guide your decision-making process, setting it in something concrete rather than allowing it to be clouded by emotion.

Identify the hazards

In many ways, we're creatures of the present and we tend to make decisions based on the information that is most resonant, closest at hand, most recent. During the COVID-19 pandemic, we've become acutely aware of what's happening around us and the constraints that have been imposed upon us. But when identifying hazards, we need to consider all the things that may have a negative impact on whatever we're trying to achieve. So, when identifying hazards don't just consider the here and now hazards but think about the potential ramifications of your decision for the future.

Assess the risks

Formal risk analysis translates technical knowledge into terms that people can use. It requires assessment against a published standard and requires advanced training and substantial resources. However, the type of risk assessment I'm talking about here is the back-of-the-envelope type calculations that can help you make sense of otherwise bewildering choices. Combined with behavioral research, risk analysis can help explain why reasonable people sometimes make different decisions. Why do some people wear face masks when out in public while others do not? Do they perceive the risks differently or are they concerned about different risks?

Making risk-based decisions are never about a single risk. For example, during the pandemic, decisions may involve trade-offs between various risks and their benefits (e.g. returning to work or school, seeing family, or travelling too far from home) or trade-offs between risks (e.g. flying versus driving). When I decided to embark upon my new career path, I had to balance the financial security of a government job against the volatility of the private sector.

If you experience a corona event and are confronted with a corona dilemma, you must then choose which path you will follow. During the COVID-19 pandemic, fear is a major influencer on our ability to make a rational decision. Research undertaken after the September 11 terrorist attacks in the U.S. found that fear heightened people's perception of risk and so, too, their intentions to take precautions. Try then to assess risk as objectively as is possible. Assess the risk of making a decision, and likewise that of not making a decision. Choosing to maintain the status quo is just as much a decision as it is deciding to change your life. Which set of risks are you willing to bear?

Make a decision

The number-one rule is to make sure you're in the right state of mind to make a rational decision. But it's important to realize that part of the reason for the decision you make will – and should be – based on your personal desires. When I chose to resign from my government job it was based on the fact that the job wasn't providing me with the satisfaction that I sought. I wanted to do something that I really enjoyed where I felt I could make a difference. This is *not* the same as being in a particular mood when you're making a decision, like my boss yelled at me so I decided to quit or a mystery thief stole my lunch from the communal fridge. When weighing up the pros and cons of your decision, remember that personal reasons may land on either side of the ledger.

Another fundamental rule about decision making is that sometimes the worst decision is not making a decision at all. When I was a flying instructor and teaching students how to fly twin-engine planes, the most critical phase was practicing engine failures immediately after takeoff at maximum takeoff weight. If you choose the wrong engine to shutdown you *will* crash. I used to say to students: "You have three choices here. One, do nothing. Two, shut down the left engine, and three, shut down the right one. And your passengers and you are only going to survive if you make the right choice."

When you've made a choice, especially one that you can't reverse, like selling your house or resigning from work, then you must have faith in your conviction and stand by that decision. No decision is perfect. Provided you've made your decision rationally and taken account of all relevant facts and ignored the irrelevant ones, then that was the best decision you could've made at that point in time. Sure, things may change after you've made your decision, but that's all in the past and all you need to focus on is the future.

Finally, it's also perfectly okay to acknowledge that you've made a mistake and to change your mind. It's also okay to make peace with your choice, even if what you chose isn't exactly what you wanted it to be. Recall from chapter one that more people regret the things they *didn't* do in life rather than having done things that could've been done better or perhaps not even done at all. No matter what, give yourself credit for having considered the possibilities and made choices that seemed rational in a time when things were confusing, frightening, and uncertain.

How to Start Thinking Differently

Thinking positively is a lot easier when things are going well. It's a lot harder when things go bad. Yet when times are tough, this is when personal or organizational change is most likely to occur. As we saw in the previous chapter, big changes bring with them big opportunities, like how my corona event led me to make big changes in my life, as did IBM when they faced serious financial difficulties. In the midst of the COVID-19 pandemic, things were certainly not going well. Let's now see an example of how times of change and crises can bring about life-changing paradigms.

Consider the story of Steven Georgiou, better known as folk and pop music icon, Cat Stevens. At the age of 15, Georgiou's father bought him a guitar and within a year he was performing at local bars. While attending Hammersmith Art College, he wrote "The First Cut Is the Deepest," sold it to soul singer, P.P. Arnold for $40, and it became a hit single on the UK charts. By 1966, Steven's star was on the rise. He changed his name to Cat Stevens, scored a record deal, had his own hit single that charted at number two, and was touring the UK with a little-known up-and-comer named Jimi Hendrix. He was living in London's West End, the epicenter of youth culture. He was just 20 years old. He had his head in the clouds and the world at his feet. But, after months of partying, drinking, smoking, and working non-stop, Stevens became gravely ill with tuberculosis and faced a year-long recuperation. This was Stevens' corona event.

Depressed about his situation and stuck in a hospital in Surrey, Stevens began thinking deeply about life and re-assessing everything. He'd always been open to seeking out influences. In an interview in *Esquire*

Middle East, he said that he had listened to everything and had picked up "all kinds of tones, tastes, and delicacies. Spanish, Russian choral or Armenian or electronic." During his recuperation period, his openness extended far beyond his musical preferences. His friend, Paul Ryan, sent him Paul Brunton's *The Secret Path*, a Buddhist text that teaches a technique of spiritual self-discovery.

Then things changed. Or rather, Cat Stevens made the conscious decision to think differently.

Stevens started seeing his time in hospital as an opportunity. There had to be something he could gain from the situation. So, he began to explore meditation and Buddhism, he turned to classical music, playing Bach over and over on a portable record player, he learned to listen deeply, and to read and write music. He also connected with his fellow patients, spending time with them in the games room and cultivating the sort of empathy and kindness that's usually difficult for a 20-year-old pop star to imagine.

Recovering from TB gave Stevens time and space to reconsider his life choices and how they aligned with his values and beliefs. He was transformed during this period of illness and recuperation, as a man and an artist. He emerged kinder, wiser, and clearer about what mattered most to him. It was during his recuperation that Cat Stevens wrote his most iconic music, the simpler, heart-felt, more authentic songs the world remembers him for.

By 1975, Cat Stevens had sold millions of records and was a global musical sensation. Incredibly, another near-death experience helped him reassess his life yet again. This time, as the story goes, Stevens was swimming at a beach in Malibu when a strong current swept him offshore. Alone and close to drowning, he prayed, calling out to God, "If you save me, I'll work for you." At that moment, a gentle wave helped carry him back to shore.

Stevens stood by his promise, finding a new path when his brother gave him a copy of the Koran. The book so deeply impacted him that he left behind the songs and persona of Cat Stevens to embrace Islam. He said of his conversion, "I found something I was so much more excited about. I didn't need to search any more in the musical world because I'd done it, I'd climbed the mountain, I was looking down and saying, 'Well, where next?'"

Cat Stevens formally embraced Islam on 4 July 1978, changing his name to Yusuf Islam. In the years since, he dedicated himself to raising a family and performing charity work. In recent years, he has returned to making music on his own terms, bringing together his great loves of faith and music.

Two near-death experiences had transformed Yusuf Islam, but it wasn't just the experiences themselves that led to the massive changes he made in his life. Rather, it was what he did with these experiences, the choices he deliberately made to take in new information and to truly listen to the world and to what his heart was telling him, that led to these profound changes. The experiences were catalysts for him to reassess his beliefs and values. He thought deeply about the decisions he had been making in life and asked: Were these decisions true to his beliefs? Was he living with intention?

Yusuf Islam's life-changing experiences represent two classic examples of a corona event leading to a corona dilemma. In each of these moments, Yusuf reflected on what was important to him, reassessed his values and beliefs, and decided what he was going to do about changing his life to protect and uphold those values and beliefs. He took in new input from the world, and rather than being passive and letting the information just wash over him, he took it to heart. He paid attention to the world and assessed his place from a position of curiosity, interest, and wonder. Yusuf wasn't concerned with the societal indoctrinations that told him to keep on the pop star path, live hard, make lots of money, and die an early death like so many of his musician colleagues. He thought like a child and applied the treasure trove of experiences he had collected over a lifetime, and he came to conclusions that he felt were right for him. And then, crucially, he acted on it.

Figure 6: The Corona Dilemma

It's easy to see how we can draw comparisons to Yusuf's experiences as there are undeniable parallels to the position that many of us have faced during the COVID-19 pandemic. When you're faced with the anxiety of your mortality, immaterial things become just that – immaterial. This explains why during times of self-isolation, many of us have become more thoughtful about what values in life *really* matter to us. We're not worrying about Maslow's higher-level needs of esteem and self-actualization when we've got physiological and safety needs that we first need to satisfy. The main reason we've become more contemplative is that we have the time and space to think.

So, Where to from Here?

In the previous chapter we saw how change is the medium for presenting us with new opportunities. One of the opportunities that change bestows upon us is the ability to change within yourself (*intra*-personal change). This is the type of change we need to start thinking differently and to approach life from a new perspective. This chapter has been all about learning *what* it is about yourself that needs to change to allow this to happen. Hence, we have learnt of how our paradigms are structured and what we need to do to undergo a paradigm shift. In the next chapter, I present a model of creativity that provides the framework for visualizing this new way of thinking – 20-20 Thinking.

Learnings from Chapter 2:

Underlying everything we do, think and believe are our paradigms that create our realities. Understanding how paradigms work helps to us understand and embrace creative thinking – change starts from within. For businesses the equivalent of personal paradigms is the organizational culture. Though it isn't always easy, it is possible to change our paradigms and corporate cultures and to start thinking more creatively. To break the habit of conformity we must be prepared to seek out influences, information, ideas, and habits that ring true. Consider the decisions you make, measure them against your newly established core values, and be willing to discard habits and ideas that aren't working.

Now go to **Chapter 6 – Habits** and relate the above learnings to the following habits:

- Habit #3: Do you need space and time to feed your soul?
- Habit #4: Do you focus intensely?

3

THE CREATIVE VISION

*"When you change the way you look at things,
the things you look at change."*

Max Planck

Back in another life, when I was a high school math teacher, I used to play games with my students; it was an unfounded optimism that it would promote that learning math could be interesting, or at least not so boring. On that occasional occasion, my optimism was blissfully rewarded. One game I would play with my students was based on numerical sequences. I'd begin the class by writing the numbers one, two, and four on the board and asking the class to identify as many different numbers as possible that could follow in sequence. I explained that with mathematical sequences, there can be many different rules you can use to base a sequence on, but I had a particular rule in mind. I challenged the class to identify *my* rule, assisting them by showing whether or not the number they volunteered would conform to my rule. As with most of my games, I offered a prize to the first student who could identify the correct answer.

I'll never forget playing this game with a particular Year 11 class at a high school that I'd recently transferred to in Sydney's northern suburbs. We were about three weeks into the term, so the students were still uncertain about what sort of teacher they thought I was. After a few minutes, I opened the floor to the students to share the numbers they had come up with. The usual responses were predictably seven and eight, with seven being an incremental increase of three, and eight being double the previous number. I then informed the class that both these numbers conformed to my rule, but neither were, in fact, *based* on my rule. I encouraged them to try and think laterally as there were still many other numbers that would fit.

After a few minutes, one student suggested five. The rest of the class looked confused. "Five," I told the class "is correct. Five conforms to my rule." The class were shocked. "But tell me," I asked the student, "what rule did you base your answer on?" To this, he replied "Sequential numbers that alternate between non-prime and prime numbers." Another student put up her hand and declared that she'd also come up with five but had a different rule. Her rule, as she explained to the class, was based on the spelling of the next number in that it had to contain four or less letters.

Two great answers that conformed to my rule, but again neither response was based on *my* rule. I was most encouraged by the last responses and I could sense that the class was becoming intriguingly interested. Then after a few more minutes, one of the girls in the front row revealed "14" as her sequential number. Her rule, as she explained; "Obviously the numbers in the sequence must all contain the letter O." Then it was on – I could almost see the creative cogs ticking in their brains that had never previously been activated during school hours, not least of which during math class.

I still remember to this day, as vividly as it happened, how, in an instant, the atmosphere in the classroom changed. There was an immediate sense of engagement and intrigue and the kind of interpersonal interaction that when a teacher experiences it, reaffirms that it truly is the most rewarding profession in the world.

After some considerable time, one of the quieter students said that her next number in the sequence was 100. The rest of the class were mesmerized. "Correct," I responded as it, too, conformed to my rule. I then asked what her rule was? She replied, "100 is bigger than the number before it."

Finally, we had a winner!

The prize I'd offered the class was that the student who got the correct answer wouldn't have to come to my next math class but would instead be commemorated with a highly sought-after library study pass. To my delight, she *did* come to my next class, and was later awarded the most improved math student of the year.

Never in my wildest dreams could I ever have imagined that this game I played with my Year 11 math class would still stick with me now. And in the scope of the right here and right now writing this book, I had never conceived that this game would help me develop a model for the creative thought process.

Over the ages, psychiatrists, behavioral psychologists and neuroscientists have espoused a myriad of hypotheses and theories as to what the creative process is all about. Nobel Prize winner, Marie Curie, believed creativity was a personality trait within us all and is developed "above all else, by having confidence in ourselves." Neuroscientists Mark Beeman and John Kounious mapped what happens in the brain during that moment of creative insight – those elusive "a-ha" moments – and found that it required the brain to be relaxed and rested and in a "diffuse" state, explaining it as a fundamental neurocognitive process. But Professor Suzanne Nalbantian, co-author of the *Secrets of Creativity: What Neuroscience, the Arts, and Our Minds Reveal* believes that creativity and the creative process is better explained in terms of various functions including "behaviorally, cognitively, and neurophysiologically."

Although it appears that there's no general consistency between these theories, this is because we've been looking at each in isolation. We're seeking a common element from the perspective of our experiences and beliefs, just as the students did in search of a common rule for the number sequence. But what we need to do to find commonality is examine things more broadly and beyond the constraints of our personal paradigms. As we're about to discover, if we allow our minds to open, we can see that these theories do have a high degree of consistency, and collectively they may reveal the secrets of the creative process.

We saw in Chapter 1 that frozen thinking is our tendency to process information in a manner that reinforces our personal beliefs, experiences, and expectations. This is when our minds are in closed mode. When the students became more and more focused on trying to identify some seemingly obscure numerical sequence, they lost sight of the obvious. It seemed the harder they tried, the less likely they were to succeed. Had this sequence challenge been presented in an art class or perhaps by a more relaxed, less conservative teacher, the obvious may have been more obvious. But being a mathematical exercise in a math class, there was a preconception or even expectation that the answer had to conform to the usual rigor of mathematical conundrums. Such is the nature of cognitive biases, as was demonstrated so dramatically with the McGurk Effect in the previous chapter. Because we engage in frozen thinking, we perceive things not as *they* are but rather as *we* are.

As we saw with our classroom challenge, it was necessary to consider the broader context to discover the rule I had for a numerical sequence. Similarly, in the construct of a model to explain the creative thought process, it's imperative that it be sufficiently expansive to encapsulate the salient features of each of these creative hypotheses. Such a model can only be developed provided it's not founded exclusively on rational construct or our experiences nor that it draws on our habitual, non-creative way of thinking. Therefore, we must delve beyond the realms of our existing paradigms in search of patterns that accommodate all the identified creative elements.

Creating Begins from Within

You'll recall from Chapter 2 that our paradigms are what dictate how we connect with the world. Our personal paradigms derive from three sources: everything we've learned, everything that's happened to us, and everything we believe. Our paradigms influence the way we perceive the world and how we, in turn, respond to those perceptions. If we follow in the Max Planck mindset, we must change the way we look at things to change the way we see the world, and the only way to change the way we look at things is to change our paradigms.

The COVID-19 pandemic was thrust upon us without our choice or consent. However, it's reductive and unhelpful to consider ourselves entirely powerless and passive within it. We couldn't stop the pandemic itself from happening, so our attention needs to turn towards what we *can* do and which balls we can catch now that they've all been thrown into the air. The world has changed, likely irrevocably so. That means we now must ask ourselves: how can we change the way we look at the world so that the world we perceive can change? This doesn't mean deluding ourselves into thinking and believing falsehoods, but if we can ask ourselves that simple question, we can reclaim even just a little power over our personal and creative manifestations that were stripped from us during the pandemic.

It's important to note here that changing the way we look at the world doesn't mean falling into the traps of conspiracy theories and skewed thinking. In fact, it means quite the opposite. While it's easy to denounce conspiracy theorists as kooks, people who fall into these traps *are* looking at the world differently and exploring alternatives to the information we've all been given, and the instinct to do so is admirable. They're taking some of the above advice, and in doing so, they've changed the way they look at the world, so their world looks different. From their perspective, upon stumbling across such new "insights," it's easy to mistake this for having woken up from the lies the world has been feeding them. However, once they take that step of looking deeper into topics that pique their curiosity and find information that contains a kernel of truth but is laden with faulty assumptions, people can sometimes get stuck there, unable to see beyond the conspiracy theory and only finding evidence that fits that theory of the world. They essentially get stuck in the same traps of frozen thinking that they were so desperately trying to free themselves of in the first place.

The same idea is a common pitfall of artificial intelligence systems. In AI, it's known as "getting stuck in the local minima" or "overfitting." In this condition, if an AI's algorithm is incomplete, incorrect, has bad data, or has wrong inputs, it will try to make sense of new information based on the faulty data and therefore try to make something fit when it actually doesn't.

In 2016, Microsoft released Tay, an AI chatbot who was designed to mimic the language interactions of a 19-year-old American girl on Twitter. When Tay was released on the social media network, the intention was that she would learn interactions based on the input she received and would respond appropriately. The internet being, well, the internet, it didn't take long before people bombarded the chatbot with inappropriate, racist, and offensive comments and material. Tay quickly learned this and, assuming this to be "normal," she began responding in equally inappropriate and racist ways. The input was skewed and faulty, and the AI algorithm over-fitted the input so it believed that was normal human interaction. And so, at only 16 hours old, Tay had to be shut down.

Conspiracy theories, too, fall into this same category. The instinct to question the world and not take things on face value is a positive one. Looking at things with deep wonder and curiosity is a great starting point for expanding your knowledge and understanding of the world and getting out of a frozen thinking mindset. Yet, it's important to also accurately assess the input received lest bad information hijack those good intentions.

In computer science, as with life, preventing overfitting can be done. Using methods like validating information with verifiable sources, consuming more and varied information, and identifying the difference between the signal (the information you're looking for) and the noise (all the extraneous information that muddies the waters) are good ways to avoid the problem. When in doubt, many computer scientists will apply the philosophical principle of Occam's Razor which suggests that when there are two explanations for something, the one that requires the least amount of assumptions is usually correct. Under these conditions, conspiracy theories too, will almost always fall apart.

It may seem odd to use conspiracy theorists as an example for change, and by no means do I support the existence of such harmful theories. However, they do serve as an example that shows how paradigm shifts can occur and how quickly they can color one's entire perception of the world. In the case of conspiracy theorists, the paradigm shift may even happen without them realizing it. As they ostracize themselves from those who disagree with their new worldview and associate more and more with a community who support it, the deeper down the rabbit hole they go. Yet imagine this in a reverse situation where it's a person who emerges from the clutches of a cult. The steep paradigm shift will need to be swift, and as they surround themselves with positive influences who support the new paradigm, the more positive the outcome. This, too, is what we need to do. To change paradigms toward something more positive, more accepting of your values, and more supportive of your goals, it will need to be a thorough and conscious decision you make that informs all subsequent decisions.

The Necessity of Structure

Before you can begin working to develop a creative idea, you need a creative rule or framework to help both facilitate ideation as well as rein in your brain's propensity for getting off-track. Although creative thinking practices want you to think outside the box and start joining disparate dots together to form new ideas, the process is quickly derailed if you start thinking about what you'll have for dinner tonight or whether you need to iron your clothes for the weekend. A framework helps to keep the ideas on track, something like a sheepdog might herd in stray sheep.

If we can learn to visualize what the creative process looks like and imagine what it would be like, then we're well positioned to make the process work for us. We do this by undergoing a creative paradigm shift founded in the acceptance of the possibility that we can change the world we perceive, and then construct the world we desire. By thinking creatively, we can create a world of opportunity and realize the reality we seek.

Our reality and paradigms are fixed within a set of conventions and values. However, there are also no limits on where creativity and imagination can take us. Only once we discover that there can be more, that we can take the camera into our own hands, change the shutter speed, and focus our lens wherever we want, do we recognize the limits of our present reality. What more can you see, visualize, create? If you were given the camera of your own vision, what would you want to photograph?

Using a model to narrow in on where you want to focus, like a camera's viewfinder, helps bring these possibilities together. By projecting your creative vision into the model, in all its many steps and variables, you can ensure that you have created for yourself the perfect atmosphere for successful creativity. Consider these models avenues of freedom of expression or thought excursions, sweeping you away on a journey of the mind. These moments of enlightenment enable you to override your cognitive biases and propensity to resort to frozen thinking.

It's important to reiterate a distinction here that while a model or structure for creativity generates a process for you to follow, this is not inherently confining. Creativity in itself champions individuality and flexibility, so a model provides a versatile method into which you can incorporate your subjective experiences and intentions. A friend of mine once worked as a crossword puzzle maker and was often asked how she came up with what words to put in a crossword. Her response was always that when she started making a new crossword, she would give herself parameters. She would say to the person asking her this question: "think of any word." The average person's vocabulary consists of 20,000-40,000 words, so to come up with any word in your entire vocabulary bank floods your mind and it goes into overload, making it harder to access something as simple as a word. "Now," she would say, "think of a word that starts with the letter G or think of a six-letter word with the second letter being E, or even, name a food you're craving right now." It's much easier to think of words that fit into these parameters while still exercising creativity.

This is what a model does. It doesn't constrict but rather gives your brain the parameters to work within and also what to explore beyond. If my friend thought of a seven-letter word or a word beginning with K to start her crossword with instead, it wouldn't matter. The self-imposed con- straints were only there to help guide her mind towards a starting point, to narrow in on what was a vast array of possibilities into something the mind can work with. That's what we're doing here – getting your mind to focus on what's important and giving it the playing field for it to start playing on.

The question we should now pose is: how can we visualize that which is hidden in our subconscious? How do we delve into our subconscious and retrieve those creative associations that can assist in providing a creative solution to our problem or the issue we are trying to resolve?

Creating Creativity: The Power of Visualization

Visualization is everything. By knowing in its entirety what your mission is, you can visualize each step needed to reach it. It can be difficult to visualize what the future looks like, when, in this post corona-world, everything appears fuzzy or undecipherable. Amidst this uncertainty, it's essential that we create our own certainties of what our goals and ambitions are.

The coronavirus crisis dramatically forced us to re-evaluate our norms of how we socialize and entertain ourselves. Perhaps never before had you considered just how much you relied on being out of the house, surrounded by other people, being close, friendly, hugging, kissing. Around the world, governments, businesses, and individuals had to quickly scramble for solutions when faced with the weight of an unknown virus infecting thousands by the day and killing hundreds. Within a matter of days, many countries, states, and cities shut down bars, restaurants, cinemas, theaters, sports clubs, and other venues for the sake of public safety. And we retreated indoors, like vampires shunning the sunlight.

This presented a problem for many parties. First, there was the everyday consumer who was seemingly lost without access to friendship groups, community, and spaces conducive of their passions. Boredom and feelings of isolation were inevitable. Thus, we collectively, as a society, emerged with a new goal: to still be entertained and feel connected, even while alone.

Secondly, there were the business owners and their employees. How were they going to maintain a profit when their usual revenue was sourced from human interaction itself? What were the bartenders to do with no bars to tend; the performers with no stage to perform on? The goal for these businesses remained the same: to engage their client base, remain relevant, profit, and to provide entertainment, relaxation and joy to a world anxious about the new unknown.

Paradigm shifts made survival for these individuals and businesses critical. Necessity has stoked creativity in these cases but passion for their business and profession has inspired them. Their goal remained ever-present. What changed, and what required creative thinking, was the avenues to reach these goals.

In many instances, online alternatives took the stage as the most promising solution. The entertainment and restaurant industries as we knew them took on an entirely new face. The list of new, virtual, and DIY alternatives is not exhaustive: webinars, online classes, DIY cook-alongs, cocktail kits, livestreamed shows, virtual museums, and so on. These businesses continued to provide the resources, packs, and educational materials for their services, but it was now at the fingertips of everyday consumers.

What we're seeing here is a proliferation in people wanting to do things for themselves. Creativity became something not just attainable, but also desirable. The appeal of making a loaf of sourdough from scratch becomes a microcosm of the burgeoning appeal of the simple, organic life. With life seemingly on pause, we no longer felt strained by the external pressures to keep up with our fast-paced world.

Much can be said about the difference between socializing in person as compared to the lag-ridden wonders of video calls. And nothing quite matches the magic of watching your favorite band perform live or meeting up with friends for a few too many glasses of wine. But we worked with the hand dealt to us. And I'd say we've done a pretty decent job.

Our present is never a constant, nor is it fixed. Once you've visualized your intended future, you begin the process to render it tangible. As

Talking Heads singer-songwriter, David Byrne, encourages us, "the future is certain, give us time to work it out." You will undoubtedly encounter barriers, but how you manage to respond and overcome these, to change your present reality, is what defines you as creative.

This is what visualization is all about. It's not solely about being swept up in grand visions of pedestals or podiums or trophies, although those are all very nice and gratifying. True success comes from process, each individual landmark between your present self and your grand creative vision. Your vision is made up of many individual visions and ideals you can reach for, step by step.

20-20 Thinking: The Complete Story

Chapter 1 provided us with a reason for change, namely, to allow us to consider the opportunities that a changed world present. Then, in Chapter 2, we examined the psychological processes associated with the type of change (intra-personal) necessary to be able to avail ourselves of these new opportunities. Now comes the hard part. Now we look at the overall cognitive processes involved with the way of thinking required to identify and realize the opportunities that our changed world presents. This includes the mental processes for acquiring knowledge and understanding through thought, experiences, and our senses. This is what we call 20-20 Thinking, a concept we touched on in Chapter 1, but now it's time to start getting up close and personal.

The very essence of 20-20 Thinking is that it's a process that enables us to attain goals through the development and implementation of creative ideas. Creative ideas allow us to become more effective in the way we resolve problems or achieve goals, and this makes us more agile in responding to our rapidly changing world. Now, more than ever, as we move to create our next normal in a world beyond COVID-19, is the time to embark upon a new way of thinking.

To better understand how to start thinking 20-20 style, it's best to begin by looking at the totality of what 20-20 Thinking is. In the Introduction, Colette Smith described 20-20 Thinking as "a collection of models and tools you can apply to approach thinking creatively about the situation you're in." The model I developed that allows for the visualization of the entirety of the 20-20 Thinking process is what I refer to as the *Creative Monk Model*. And the tool that I've developed to assist us in engaging in 20-20 Thinking is the C-R-E-A-T-E process. In Chapters 4 and 5, we'll learn to apply this model and use this tool to allow you to start changing the way you think. Finally, in Chapter 6 we will look at the habits that support this type of thinking so that it becomes the norm for your next normal.

In the remainder of this chapter, we'll start reviewing the C-R-E-A-T-E process and in the next chapter take a look at the Creative Monk Model. But before we do that, there are a few things about 20-20 Thinking that you should know. The first is that 20-20 Thinking is *not* an alternative to the type of rational and intuitive thinking modes that we touched on in the previous chapter. 20-20 Thinking is in fact an additional way of thinking. It's a mode of thinking that we can evoke when we want to explore creative solutions to resolve specific and predetermined, problems or concepts.

In Chapter 1, we looked at frozen thinking and our tendency to process information in a manner that reinforces our personal beliefs, experiences, and expectations. Because of this cognitive bias, *all* our thinking – both rational and intuitive – is subconscious. This means that the thinking processes we applied in our pre-COVID-19 world will be the same and will accompany us to our next normal _unless_ we make a conscious decision to change the way we think. Because frozen thinking constrains how we process information, the only way to move forward is to unshackle the impediments that keep our thoughts firmly rooted in our familiar environment. To come up with creative ideas based neither on experience nor expectations, we need to start thinking differently. This is why we need 20-20 Thinking. If there were ever an opposite to frozen thinking, then this is it.

Typically, we all operate in two different types of thinking modes – thinking fast and thinking slow. When we need to think fast, our rational mind is in a highly focused state and operating in closed mode. In resolving problems, our mind searches for the most familiar solution, which are invariably the least creative. On the other hand, when we're thinking slow, our mind is open, and we're generally in a more relaxed mood, more intuitive, and open to explore novel ideas. The fast thinking mind, however, has the advantage that it uses far less energy in resolving a situation. Both these modes of thinking serve worthwhile purposes and civilization seems to have survived thus far without even the contemplation of an addition thinking mode.

By way of example to demonstrate our need for both these ways of thinking, consider the following: You've just received your end-of-year exam results. You weren't sure which way they'd go, but you passed so you're feeling quite relieved. Either way they'd gone, you'd resolved to go out celebrating – hard. And so, you did. The next morning, slightly worse for wear, you need a pick-me-up. In this moment, your mind is very much in closed mode, so you order the usual – a double expresso and a bacon and egg burger. Now's not the time to experiment with novel solutions, so the thought of a piccolo latte with half-skinny extra foam and a gherkin sandwich doesn't even get a look in. Sometimes, we need quick solutions using minimal brain power just to get the job done.

The final, and most important point about 20-20 Thinking is that it's really not a new type of thinking. And to observe 20-20 Thinking in action, all we need to do is to look under our noses – metaphorically and literally. Children are incredibly creative thinkers. They imagine without any of the limitations that adults put on our thinking. Children are divergent thinkers capable of producing a range of ideas — freely, generously, and without an inner critic taking notes. Yet as adults, we tend to view a mistake as failure instead of a natural and essential part of the creation process. A child-like mindset (notably, as opposed to a child*ish* mindset) can facilitate our ability to engage in 20-20 Thinking. Children start every day with excitement and curiosity, they continually question why things are as they are and play games to explore the new ideas about the world that awaits them.

If you take a quick look at the Creative Assessment Test in Chapter 6, you'll see the extent to which children, every day, practice the habits that support 20-20 Thinking. Children continually challenge the way the world is (Habit 1), they're forever curious about why things are the way they are (Habit 2), they think and speak in pictures and images (Habit 5), they're totally unconcerned about what other people think about what they do (habit 7), they have a mind that rarely slows down (Habit 8), and, of course, they think and behave like a child (Habit 10), because that's who they are.

So, how do we start thinking like kids? As Albert Einstein once said, "To stimulate creativity, one must develop the childlike inclination for play." Remember those endless, summer playdays of your childhood? When your imagination was in full flow, you'd magic whole worlds from boxes, populate cities with flying monsters, and make the impossible a reality. But remember, no-one has exclusive ownership over creativity – not even children. Yet as adults, we lock ourselves into linear ways of life, denying ourselves that rich freedom of imagination. Unlike adults, children solve problems in a non-linear fashion, their bowerbird imaginations collecting, sorting, and rearranging all those glittering daydreams into a nonsensical world that they live in and treasure.

While all this sounds like child's play, let me tell you, if your think that growing up was rough, then I'd suggest you don't underestimate what it takes to grow down. There's some serious rewiring of your brain required here. The frontal cortex of the brain is responsible for cognitive skills, including problem-solving, language, and process-driven behavior. As we enter our early 20s, the frontal cortex becomes more "rational," allowing us to make value judgments and decisions based largely on past experiences. The downside to this neurological process is that we start to lose our ability for divergent thinking, which is a major impediment to creativity.

The remainder of this chapter will look at what's required for us to start the process of rewiring our brain so we can engage in 20-20 Thinking. I'll explain and highlight the importance of process, and we'll also learn how to prime our brain so our subconscious can do some of the heavy creative lifting.

So, let's start with the process.

The C-R-E-A-T-E Process

For a creative concept to progress to reality, we must clearly understand the creative process so it can be replicated and effectively implemented through the practice of creative habits. Recall from the beginning of this chapter how my Year 11 students found it difficult to try and find a common rule for a sequence of numbers. They failed because they had no structure or process to follow. Sometimes the "obvious" is the hardest to see and the first to be overlooked. The underlying message in providing a phased approach to developing a creative mindset is the insistence upon the importance of process. A step-by-step methodology greatly assists in ensuring that you can achieve complex undertakings and that no critical items are overlooked. This is why airline pilots rely on checklists. How many times have you seen footage of a plane that arrives at a runway with the pilot having forgotten to lower the undercarriage? Flying an airliner is not a simple endeavor; nor is learning to think differently.

Subsequent chapters will deal with the C-R-E-A-T-E process in much finer detail. For now, I'd like to give you a brief introduction to this handy acronym.

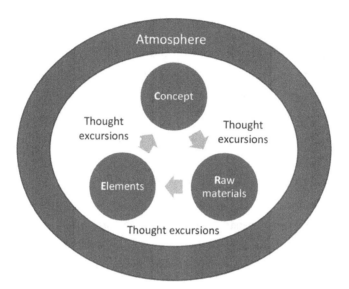

Figure 7: The C-R-E-A-T-E Process

Concept – The concept is the big picture, devoid of detail. Steve Jobs described a similar thing as "the idea, the problem, or the wrong that you want to right." It's the idea of being in a new career, not *which* job you'll land; it's the new relationship you'll form, not *what* relationship; it's the new marketing strategy, not *what* the strategy will be, and so on. By undertaking the six-step creative process, the concept will be modified as and when new creative elements develop.

Raw materials: Raw materials are the pieces of information you collect to explore a concept. It encompasses the three 'R's of creativity: Recall, Research, and Reach out. *Recall* requires you to access pieces of information floating in your head, and identify and write down noteworthy points, ideas or experiences. These become your "creative skyhooks" or the "dots" that you want to join with other "dots." *Research* is then needed so you can find out more about the important parts or background of your concept. The last stage asks you to *reach out* and share your ideas and concept with others on the premise that a good idea doesn't care who's had it.

Elements – These are the building blocks of creative concepts. Just as base elements make up compounds in nature, creative elements are the building blocks for creative concepts. When associated relationships come together and form a bond, they create an *element* that in some way relates to the concept. The formation of elements is the "ah-ha" moments of the creative process. These elements then become part of the concept and may modify or further develop the concept.

The ***creative triad*** consists of the three base components of the creative process: **C–R–E** or *Concept – Raw materials – Elements*. Concepts either develop outward or focus inward with the continual flow of ideas that lead to the formation of elements. These three components continually interact subconsciously within the confines of our creative atmosphere.

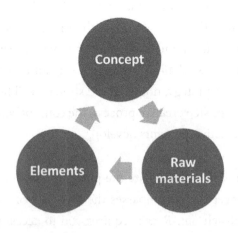

Figure 8: The Creative Triad: C–R–E

Atmosphere: Setting the scene and forming the right creative environment is extremely important. The right atmosphere allows you to let your mind off its leash and start exploring without its usual inhibitions. Creativity is all about subtraction, so creating the right atmosphere becomes about removing distractions and disruptions and inviting creativity in.

Thought excursions –– These are the subconscious thinking processes that facilitate you joining the dots between ideas, concepts, raw materials, and anything else floating around in your head. It's best to consider *thought excursions* as the process by which our subconscious mind continually processes streams of information. Thought excursions must be conducted in a different atmosphere from the conscious thinking that takes place when we formulate our concept and gather raw materials.

Thought excursions can happen when we're awake but can also occur when we're asleep. In both situations, it's when our conscious mind is in a relaxed state and we're in a good mood. Thought excursions are a habit of the mind, and this, combined with the learning of other creative habits leads to a search for relationships or associations between facts and elements. It becomes of the highest importance in the production of ideas and is the essence of creating creativity.

Execution – *Execution* is the final act of transforming concepts into reality. It's when the creative process returns to the real world. Execution is in itself can be considered as a complete process and although it is not depicted in Figure 7 it is a most important component of the C-R-E-A-T-E process. As in real life, you can take the execution of a concept as either the beginning or the end of the process. A great idea can fail because it has not been properly executed. The ultimate success or otherwise of a creative concept or idea comes down to its execution.

Process Is Critical

Creativity is a process. It's a process of developing original ideas that have value. In the '60s, a young psychologist named Sarnoff Mednick thought he had identified the essence of creativity. In his paper published in the *Psychological Review*, Mednick defined the creative thought process as:

> **▮▮** *"The forming of associative elements into new combinations which either meet specified requirements or are in some way useful. The more mutually remote the elements of the new combination, the more creative the process or solution."*

The inclusion of the requirement that such a process yields something "useful" differentiates *creative* thinking from mere *original* thinking. Thus, 7,363,474 is an original answer to the problem "how much is 12 + 12?" However, we can only call this creative when conditions are such that the answer is useful – that it provides an opportunity to create something functional. If we return to the challenge that was presented to my Year 11 math class, a response of 7,363,474 could legitimately be considered as both original *and* creative in conforming with my rule that it's a number greater than the previous number. With the imposition of a rule for this challenge, we also introduce a framework where creativity can be created.

As a logical progression, what we can now assert is that what many people and businesses lack is not creative potential, but rather that they're devoid of any framework where they can focus and unleash their creative talent. So, it's crucial to establish a model or framework that encompasses and portrays the totality of whatever concept or goal you're attempting to realize. Once you've developed such a model, then, and only then, can you develop the processes to transform your concept into reality.

When we're considering developing a model that can provide an alternative way of seeing the world, it must include a representation of the creative process. This applies equally to personal goals and business processes. Suppose, for instance, that you have a business with mature business practices that supports practically every aspect of the enterprise, from business resilience to having a corporate travel policy that details employees' acceptable usage of hotel minibars while on work assignments. But where is the system or process for developing and managing creativity within the workplace? The most important thing that a business should do is left to pure chance. Managers take creativity for granted yet wonder why they're missing opportunities that arise from a rapidly changing commercial environment. At the personal or corporate level, without a structured process for developing and nurturing creativity, the prospects of an idyllic outcome simply occurring are significantly diminished.

Creativity is something we must create for ourselves. With a defined framework for creating creativity, process becomes an essential methodology on two levels. First, process defines the essence of creativity. Creativity isn't a happening or an event; it's a process. Secondly, process is essential to the art of doing creativity. Altogether, we recognize creativity as an act, and not merely something static or abstract. To create, we need to do creative things which require us to develop creative habits. Creative habits support the creation of creativity – not the other way around. Process at this level is equally important and relates to the development and reinforcement of creative habits. We explore more about the nature of creative habits in Chapter 6 and what we can do to change negative habits or to adopt positive new ones.

In 1939, James Webb Young, an American advertising executive, wrote a short treatise titled *A Technique for Producing Ideas*. Young was a voraciously curious and cross-disciplinary thinker at heart, and in his publication, he set out what he considered as the essential steps of the creative process. Focusing on several elements in the process – all of which have since been corroborated by science – Young's enduring legacy and key contribution to the development of creative realization is his insistence on process over any innate creative talents.

In developing a model of creativity, it must incorporate and demonstrate how we process information so that it emerges in the form of fresh new combinations, associations, and relationships. The model must also depict how this processing occurs at different levels within our brain's cognitive systems. Scientists commonly distinguish activity in our conscious mind as between rational thinking and intuitive thinking, with a significant proportion of intuitive thinking taking place at the subconscious level. Einstein considered intuition as the only path to new insights in stating, "I never made one of my discoveries through the process of rational thinking." Young, however, goes one step further and connects the intuitive with the practical and experiential dimension.

> "The production of ideas is just as definite a process as the production of Fords; that the production of ideas, too, runs on an assembly line; that in this production the mind follows an operative technique which can be learned and controlled; and that its effective use is just as much a matter of practice in the technique as is the effective use of any tool."

Neuroscience confirms that highly creative people think and act differently than the average person because they practice creative habits. They have trained their brains to habitually do creative things. James Young provides some helpful insights into the nature of creative implementation strategies:

> *"In learning any art the important things to learn are, first, principles, and second, method. This is true of the art of producing ideas. Particular bits of knowledge are nothing, because they are made up of, so called, rapidly aging facts. Principles and method are everything."*

So, for Young, in the art of producing ideas, what is most important to know is not where to look for a particular idea, but rather how to train the mind in the process of ideation and how to understand and apply a model that shows where all our creative ideas come from.

The most compelling aspect of Young's treatise builds on the work of Italian sociologist Vilfredo Pareto and his 1916 book, *The Mind and Society*. Young proposes two key principles for creating creativity:

1. An idea must be a new combination
2. The ability to generate new combinations depends on the ability to see relationships between different elements.

Young's first principle is that an idea is nothing more nor less than a new combination of old elements. In the foreword to his book, Bill Bernbach, the original Mad Man and founder of the advertising agency, DDB, captured the essence of Young's ideas when he proclaimed that "creativity is just connecting things."

The second principle is that the capacity to bring old elements into new combinations depends largely on our ability to see relationships or associations. This is the area of research that Mednick specialized in. Mednick's idea was as simple as it was powerful: "creativity is associative memory that works exceptionally well." Here is where our minds differ to the greatest degree when it comes to describing and visualizing the creative process. To some minds, each fact is a separate bit of information. To others, it's a link in a chain of information, it has relationships and similarities. It's not so much a fact as it is an illustration of a general law applying to a whole series of facts. 20-20 Thinking, with both its model of creativity and the C-R-E-A-T-E process, accommodates both these neurological pathways to enable creative realization.

Thought Excursions

To come up with creative solutions, we first need to escape the clutches of frozen thinking. To do so, we have to let our minds wander to a place beyond our conscious surrounds and away from the lure of our comfort zone. We have to venture into the world of our subconscious.

Thought excursions are explorations into that which is creatively possible and usually way beyond the extremities of what you know and the paradigms you keep. You need to keep pushing the envelope, testing and probing to break through the boundaries of the tried and familiar, and thought excursions are a visualization technique that puts your mind in a state that's open and ready for all kinds of creative flights of fancy. For us to more fully understand the nature of the creative thought process we must appreciate that in order to arrive at new solutions and consider different ways of doing things, we must learn new things. But how we learn new things isn't entirely straight forward and integrating them into the field of things we already know is a complicated process requiring both the conscious and subconscious mind.

As previously stated, a great deal of information processing happens in the subconscious mind, and to emphasize conscious thinking at the expense of subconscious processing in the 20-20 Thinking process would be a mistake. Einstein himself has said, "I have no doubt that our thinking goes on for the most part without the use of symbols, and, furthermore, largely unconsciously." Although creative imaginings are within the realm of our consciousness, thought excursions occur at the subconscious level and are an integral component of the overall creative thought process.

There is a dilemmic problem with our paradigms. The crux of our conundrum lies in the fact that our paradigms predispose us to what we see, or do not see. The COVID-19 pandemic belongs in the latter category. The pandemic absolutely blindsided us all. How, then, do we react? Creativity has always been important, but now on a universal, objective scale, it is absolutely imperative.

The information we acquire throughout life and the ideas we develop have a direct effect on how we perceive the world and how we relate to the world. When an idea or learning breaks into our consciousness, it wraps itself in the form of what we already know so it can be absorbed in a palatable form. This means that our paradigms determine the way we process these new learnings and pushes us into the trap of frozen thinking.

Therefore, if we become conscious of *what* and *how* we're thinking, then we can create an independent framework where we can monitor our thought processes. The real difficulty in constructing such a model of creativity is that the subconscious is where the overwhelming majority of our creative ideas are developed, but it's not readily accessible to our conscious thought processes. So, we need to train ourselves to think beyond the realms of the thinkable, the plausible, and the possible. We must embark upon a flight to a land of possibilities, to a land where the seemingly impossible become plausible realities. We must participate in thought excursions.

The subconscious was of great fascination to Sigmund Freud. He believed that as children, we use play to express our creativity and imagination. We share our feelings freely with others and enact our fantasies without self-consciousness. As adults, Freud believed that we substitute imaginative play with daydreaming. But John Cleese believes that this playful mode can also manifest as adults. According to Cleese, it's a mood in which curiosity for its own sake can operate because we're not under pressure to get a specific thing done quickly. We can play, and that's what allows our natural creativity to come to the surface.

Think of thought excursions as a journey inside the mind that follows a thought as it takes you somewhere you may not have been before. This integral part of the 20-20 Thinking process can be traced back to the beginnings of some of Albert Einstein's most famous discoveries. Ever since he was a child, Einstein would lose himself in what others would observe as daydreams. Einstein's mind was at play when he embarked upon his classic flight of consciousness thought experiment. This is something Einstein started thinking about when he was 16. By imagining what it would be like to ride on a beam of light helped him develop his theory of special relativity. If you could somehow catch up to the light, Einstein reasoned, you would be able to observe the light frozen in space. But light can't be frozen in space, otherwise it would cease to be light. Eventually Einstein realized that light cannot be slowed down and must always be moving away from him at the speed of light. Therefore, something else had to change. Einstein reasoned that time itself had to change, which laid the groundwork for his published theory of special relativity a decade later.

What makes Einstein remarkable was knowing what to do with that image of surfing the light. By merely imagining it, Albert's creative thinking was elevated to the insights and understandings of how light and time are related. From those creative imaginings came his world-famous theories in quantum physics.

The reason 20-20 Thinking borrows from Einstein's thought experiments is that the ability to take the conditions of the world around you and combine them with the widest reaches of the imagination is both incredibly valuable and within anyone's grasp. By stretching beyond the known and the possible, Einstein challenged the status quo and looked at things in ways no one previously had. Science has repeatedly proved wrong those who deny the possibility of the impossible. Only a year before the Wright brothers first flew their Wright's Flyer, Simon Newcomb, physicist and Director of the U.S. Naval Observatory, said "flight by machines heavier than air is impractical and insignificant, if not utterly impossible." Nelson Mandela got it right when he remarked "it always seems impossible until it's done."

At the personal level, consider thought excursions as a broad approach that you can tailor to pursue new ideas in any field, whether it be a ground-breaking way of doing business, the next revolutionary art movement, or the idea of ever being happy again after the loss of a loved one. Our not-so-distant relatives would've considered concepts such as space travel, organ transplants, personal computers, and paying for goods by swiping a piece of plastic utterly impossible. But Leonardo Da Vinci explored the possibility of helicopters almost half a millennium before they were invented. Thought excursions are explorations into that which is creatively possible and usually far beyond the extremities of what you know and the paradigms you keep. You need to keep pushing the envelope, testing and probing to break through the boundaries of the tried and familiar. Where creative imaginings are within the realm of our consciousness, thought excursions occur at the subconscious level but are an integral component of the overall creative thought process.

We can approach thought excursions in a multitude of ways, but my Creative Monk Model – which we explore in the next chapter – is one I've designed to deliberately target the creativity circuits of our mind and start training ourselves to think using a creative mindset.

We Are Not Born Creative

Since the turn of the new millennium, scientists have made great strides in neuroscience in providing answers to how our brains engage in creative thinking and how we can nurture it. Empirical evidence has revealed that creativity is a quality of the mind, not an inherent characteristic or specific activity.

The upshot of all this research is that it reveals that we are not born with a creative disposition. We are not born with that figurative light bulb on top of our head. Creativity is a real cognitive process where we transform the streams of information and ideas into something useful. We become creative if we do things in a manner that align with, and support, our creative thought processes. This is how we align the left brain – the artistry – with the right brain – the logical processing. Contrary to popular belief, these two sides of the brain are not entirely distinguishable from one another. A model, in incorporation of your subjective creative vision, is the absolute best avenue to create creativity.

In most instances, our brain does mental calculations from the top down with the brain's high-level executive structures dictating the approach. This is what happens when we undertake complex tasks or are focused on a specific problem. But this approach cannot solve problems if the solutions lie beyond the realm of rational deduction or logical analysis. And it cannot solve problems if the solutions do not align with our personal paradigms.

In the large body of contemporary research in the field of neuroscience, one quality stands out above all others. Unlike rational or logical reasoning, creative thinking arises from what scientists call bottom-up processes. Due to the unique architecture of the human brain, we can also perform calculations from the bottom-up. In the bottom-up mode of processing, individual neurons fire in a complex fashion without direction from an executive, but with valuable input from the brain's emotional centers and as drawn upon our intuition. This kind of processing is non-linear and can produce ideas out of left field that wouldn't otherwise have arisen in a step-by-step progression of analytical thinking.

Austin Kleon wrote in *Steal Like an Artist*:

> ▌▌ *"The creative thought process and the living of a creative lifestyle is not a linear excursion to a finish line, it's a loop, which when repeated through the exercise of creative habits, enhances the chances of encountering creative experiences. And these experiences, when meaningfully directed, can lead to a better way of doing things - and the enablers to live a better life."*

Although the creative thought process is non-linear and may appear illogical at times, this doesn't mean that adhering to a process is any less important. So, if we understand the importance of each component in the creative thought process and how they interplay, we will be sufficiently informed (and, hopefully, motivated by curiosity) to gain the knowledge and understanding required to develop the personal habits conducive to the promotion of creative thinking.

I've used Albert Einstein a lot in examples throughout this book already (and, spoiler alert: there will be plenty more to come), however, what stands out above all in his summations of his process of creative thinking is the critical role of visual imagery as opposed to words. He stated that he thought in a stream of pictures and images and insisted that visualization could be enhanced with practice until it's rich and vivid like watching a movie in your head. Einstein maintained that the application of logic and the use of words were useful when it comes to developing concepts and their execution but were ineffective when attempting to explain the concepts and realizing creative breakthroughs. Einstein then concluded, "We can't solve problems by using the same kind of thinking we used when we created them."

Now it's your turn.

Learnings from Chapter 3:

It is essential to always maintain a clear creative vision at the forefront of your creative endeavor, particularly one free from the constraints of frozen thinking, empowered in brand new perceptions. Visualize what the end creative goal looks like, then visualize what each of the steps towards it looks like. Use this to motivate your process.

Now go to **Chapter 6 – Habits** and relate the above learnings to the following habits:

- Habit #5 Do you think and speak in pictures and images?
- Habit #6 If you are passionate about something will you see it through no matter whatever it takes?

4

THE C-R-E-A-T-E PROCESS

"Our progress, the realization of our dreams,
and the quality of our life depend directly
on the level of our commitment to the process."

Dr. Prem Jagyasi

The name Elon Musk probably rings a few bells. Perhaps you think of Tesla and electric cars, or maybe of SpaceX, rocket ships, and living on Mars. Maybe you saw an article about the name of his first child, X Æ A-XII. In 2020, he ranked number 18 on Forbes' Most Powerful People in The World list, and in 2020 he came in at number 31 on Forbes' World's Billionaires list. Whatever you think of Elon Musk, he's a pretty big deal. That power and wealth has been self-made, accumulated through pursuing his own creative ideas. He is a personified exemplar of someone who uses the creative process to achieve their visions.

What's fundamentally different about Musk is the way he thinks. He describes himself as thinking from "first principles," which he defines as "boiling things down to their fundamental truths and working from there" rather than "thinking by analogy." He explains how this way of thinking led him to start SpaceX.

> ▐▐ *"Reasoning by analogy, like in the rocket business, you would say: So how much do rockets cost? Well, on average they cost, let's say, $100 million. So, therefore, your rocket will cost $100 million. Now reasoning from first principles you would say: What is a rocket made of? What are the engines made of? How are they constructed? The materials, manufacturing processes, all that and you would build that up to say, 'Okay, well, what could a rocket cost if it were done right?' And then you find, 'Oh wow a rocket could cost, like, one-tenth of that . . . the problem is that people are putting rockets together in really dumb ways.' And then you just have to be a detective and get rid of the dumb ways, and then it is much better."*

Conversely, Elon describes reasoning by analogy as "basically copying what others do with very minor incremental changes and not actually understanding why that thing was even successful in the first place." He highlights that there is nothing wrong with this mode of thinking and that it's necessary for many of the decisions we make in everyday life. However, when there's a specific goal you want to achieve or concept you wish to explore, then reasoning by analogy is not the kind of thinking that will be most effective. What you need to do is think function, not form. This doesn't just apply to scientific inventions either. It can be applied to any goal: whether it's a career goal, a goal for your company, a relationship goal, a goal for the household choices, or any other goal you may wish to achieve.

It's tempting to look at someone like Elon Musk and think that he was just born a creative genius. But while the way he perceives the world may come naturally to him, anyone can learn to think using the type of thinking – which I call 20-20 Thinking – to produce creative solutions to the problems that we face in life. The reason why this type of thinking comes naturally to Elon is because he has developed the habits that support and promote this type of thinking. So, let's begin by trying to understand more about how this type of thinking relates to the C-R-E-A-T-E process and how, in turn, you can use this method to generate creative solutions.

Thinking from First Principles

Fundamental and integral to the entire 20-20 Thinking process is the concept of thinking by first principles. Aristotle is believed to have coined the term and defined it as "the first basis from which a thing is known." It means starting from the question: What do I know to be fundamentally true? Then you can work from there to determine a solution. The opposite of thinking from first principles is reasoning by analogy, where a problem is solved by drawing conclusions based on existing examples and assumptions and finding similarities between the ideas.

Thinking by analogy often sounds like:

* "If it ain't broke, don't fix it"
* "We've always done it this way, so it must be good"
* "People would never do that."

Blogger Tim Urban has a helpful analogy for these two methods of reasoning. He contrasts the chef (who thinks from first principles) with the cook (who reasons by analogy). Chefs invent recipes. Their first principles are their raw ingredients which they then combine in unexpected ways to create new delicious dishes. Cooks follow recipes from chefs they like or recipes that lots of people have rated highly online because they know the recipe is likely to work and will produce a good dish. Like Musk, Urban also emphasizes that there's nothing wrong with being a cook.

Using first principles is hard and takes time and effort. It would be impossible to use it all the time. So, when should you be using this type of thinking? Well, this is a big kind of thinking, so you want to use it whenever you have big problems or big visions that you want to achieve. Presuming that you're reading this book to think more creatively, whenever you want creative solutions or something a bit left of center, then you need to put your chef hat on and think using first principles. While it does sound like more effort to engage in this process, it's better to sacrifice your time and effort in this process now to accomplish more in the long term.

With COVID-19, the future seems more uncertain and overwhelming than ever. By being proactive and investing in searching for creative solutions, you can take control of your future rather than letting it control you. No more following the herd into the future.

The Creative Triad, or the C-R-E of the C-R-E-A-T-E process, is all about thinking from first principles. This chapter will focus on taking you through the C-R-E of the process and give you a clear framework that you can apply so you can engage in 20-20 Thinking.

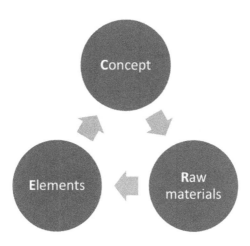

Figure 9: The Creative Triad: C-R-E

The most important component of the Creative Triad is the concept. For Steve Jobs, the concept was "the idea, the problem, or the wrong that you want to right." This is the starting point of any creative endeavor and what drives us to discover creative solutions and to transform our concepts – whatever they may be – into reality. But, as Steve Jobs insists, if you're not passionate enough from the start and not "burning" with an idea, problem, or wrong you want to right, then "you'll never stick it out."

Let's look at the three steps involved in the Creative Triad to ignite that fire within.

Step 1. Identify your **concept** – challenge assumptions to find your fundamental truth

Step 2. Gather **raw materials** – the 3 R's of creativity; research, reach out and recall

Step 3. Form the **elements** – joining the dots, the "ah-ha" moments

Step 1: Identify your Concept

As explained in the previous chapter, the C in the C-R-E-A-T-E process is for **concept**. The beginning of any creative process requires you to first identify your concept or vision. Psychologist and author, Edward de Bono highlights that the reason we often lack good ideas or fail to solve problems is because we're confused and distracted by all the different problems and solutions that exist and that we miss the most important ones. Steve Jobs identified that the reason Apple experienced a slump in 1997 was because they were focusing on too many projects at once and so failed to deliver vision on any one of them.

In a Reddit AMA chat, Elon Musk explained that "it is important to view knowledge as sort of a semantic tree — make sure you understand the fundamental principles, i.e. the trunk and big branches, before you get into the leaves/details or there is nothing for them to hang on to." In this analogy, the concept is like the trunk. It's the part of the tree that everything else relies upon. If it's not sturdy, then the branches and the leaves won't stick (no pun intended) either.

The first step you need to take is to determine what is the problem or idea that's most important for you to generate your concept. There's nothing fancy about this approach – all it requires is a statement that begins with the words "I want..." followed by whatever is important to you. There's no magic formula to this, although there are some things to avoid, which we'll look at later. While sometimes your concept jumps out at you right away, other times it can be hard to identify what your concept is. Problems can feel a bit like spaghetti – it's hard to pick up one issue without getting seven others on your fork. It's the same with ideas – there are so many good things out there, it can be hard to know which one you *really* want.

The process of visualization is incredibly important to help you formulate your concept. Later in this chapter, I introduce the *Creative Monk Model* which will help you visualize the entire 20-20 Thinking process. But for now, let's look at three visualization techniques to assist you in developing your concept. Before we begin, it's best to engage in what I call a whiteboard exercise. Picture all of your thoughts, worries, hopes, and dreams on a whiteboard and then imagine yourself rubbing them all out and leaving the board blank. Creative thinking is all about thinking afresh. This can assist in making sure your decisions aren't anchored in previous paradigms or beliefs.

Strategy 1: Visualize your identity

> *If you want to know where you should go, it's useful to first work out who you are, as your identity informs your values and your values define the direction of your concept. In the book* Work Smarter Not Harder, *authors Jack Collis and Michael LeBoeuf suggest that you can visualize who you are by writing at least 10 statements about yourself starting with "I am…" and putting each statement on a different card or piece of paper. For example, you might write, "I am a mom," or "I am an engineer," or "I am a hard worker." Once you have a collection, the authors suggest ordering these statements in order of importance to you. Start by placing the statements in three categories: most important, moderately important, and least important, and then go from there. This will tell you what aspects of your identity are most important to you and can form the basis of what area of your life should form the basis of your concept.*

Strategy 2: Visualize your future

> ▌▌ If you were to imagine your life 20 years from now, what would you like it to look like? Write it down or draw it out. This is known as a biographical technique because you're essentially writing your future biography. Once you have a vision for how you want your future to be, you can identify what's important in the present so you can achieve your ideal future. You can then formulate your future aspirations into concept statements.

Strategy 3: Visualize your worries

> ▌▌ If you find you have a lot on your mind - which would be of little wonder during a pandemic - it may be easier for you to visualize all of the issues that you worry about or cause you stress. Similar to the first strategy, by writing each of those issues down and organizing them from the most important to least important, you force yourself to determine what is the key issue. You can then reframe that key issue into a concept statement. For example, say your problem is that there isn't enough traffic on your website. You can reframe that issue into this concept: I want to see more traffic on my website. Or perhaps your problem is more personal: I feel the relationship with my partner is breaking down. This can be reframed into the concept: I want to improve the relationship with my partner.

Common mistakes in identifying your concept

Ultimately there's only one mistake that you can make when identifying your concept: identifying a concept that isn't really important to you or that doesn't align with your values. If you lack the desire for your concept, then you'll lack the drive to invest the necessary time and energy to follow through with it. In other words, you'll never ignite that fire within that Steve Jobs insists is essential to enable your concept to become a reality.

Don't panic about getting it wrong! If you realize your concept isn't really something you're invested in, you can always change direction. The beauty of the C-R-E-A-T-E process is that it incorporates modifying your concept from the one you initially started with because it assumes that as you question your assumptions and make new associations that you'll want to change your original idea. For example, if your concept started out as "I want a new job" but through the C-R-E process this may develop to become "I want a more challenging and satisfying job." So, whereas your first concept statement required you to find a *new* job the modified version keeps open the opportunity, for instance, of negotiating your dream job with your current employer. This reinforces the need to think "function" rather than "form." The realization of your concept is securing a challenging and satisfying job so you should not restrict your options as to where that job may be found.

While you're busy formulating your concept statement, here are some questions to ask yourself to keep you on track:

- Are you letting other people define your concept? I'm sure at some point you've felt the pressure of needing to conform to the expectations of others, whether it's your family, employer, spouse, colleagues, or friends. But your concept has to be *yours* – otherwise it won't be important enough to you, and it will hinder the process.

- Are you missing an important value or aspect of your life? Often when we brainstorm our goals for the future, we fail to identify all the objectives that are important to us because we think too narrowly. Talking to other people about your concept or cross-referencing your concept with a master list of different categories can ensure that you've considered all areas of your life and all the values that are important to you. This ensures that your concept is what you *really* want. This checklist outlines some common areas you might want to consider, and common goals associated with those areas, but yours will likely differ.

- o **Career:** Start your own business, get a pay rise, get promoted, change careers, further education
- o **Relationship/social**: Repair a relationship, spend more time with your children, go on more regular date nights, strengthen a friendship
- o **Health:** Sleep more, start a new sport, get fit, manage a condition
- o **Leisure:** Learn a new skill, spend time on a hobby, achieve work-life balance
- o **Business:** Create a new product, capture a proportion of market, innovate an old product, adopt new technologies, employ more diverse people.

Figure 10: Checklist of Common Concepts

- Are you focusing too much on the *how* and not the *what*? Often the difficulty when thinking big picture is that your critical rational brain comes in and tells you all the reasons why that idea won't work or isn't realistic. It's important at this stage of the thinking process that nothing is abandoned or shut out. Creative solutions often seem foolish or unrealistic at the beginning – otherwise they would already be done.

- Are you choosing a concept beyond your control? The whole point of this process is that you achieve something important to you or resolve a pressing issue. In other words, you want an outcome. However, if you choose a concept that is reliant upon external events rather than those within the scope of your influence, then you will become discouraged because no matter how hard you research, reach out, or analyze your ideas, you'll never realize your concept. Examples of these kinds of concepts are things like: I want my kid to make good life choices, or I want to be popular, or I want the Vikings to win the Super Bowl.

Identify the obstacles

I don't have to provide many tips for how to identify the obstacles to your concept because the human brain always finds it easier to think negatively – it's hardwired that way. The important thing is to write any and every obstacle that comes to mind. Hold nothing back.

Generally speaking, there are two kinds of obstacles: mental barriers and real barriers. Mental barriers can include things like motivating yourself to go to the gym or to write more blog posts. A real barrier can be something like not having the money to afford a gym membership or living far away from your workplace. It's important to be honest with yourself at this stage.

Once you've brainstormed your obstacles, collate your responses so you have a discrete list of the main obstacles.

Let's look at the examples we used in the previous section about our website and our partner – what are some of the obstacles we can identify to achieving these concepts?

If your concept was, I want more traffic on my website, then some of the obstacles could include:

- The website lacks relevant content to users
- The website doesn't rank high enough on Google searches
- The website hasn't been advertised or shared sufficiently to users.

If your concept was, I want to improve the relationship with my partner, then obstacles here might include:

- I don't spend enough time with my partner
- I don't seem to be able to communicate with my partner
- I don't share as much in common with my partner these days

Now that you have your key concepts and obstacles, we can get to the tricky yet most important part of the creative process: challenging the limits that we think we know.

Challenge your assumptions

Challenging assumptions about our concept is important because assumptions shape our reality. Assumptions are not always bad but are often necessary. We assume that cars will stop at red lights and go at green lights. We assume that we cannot breathe underwater. However, unchallenged assumptions are the enemy of first principles and creative thinking. By challenging your assumptions so you're left only with first principles, these fundamental truths will enable you to see new possibilities and generate creative ideas to achieve your concept.

You can challenge your assumptions in many different ways, and depending on the way you think and learn, some methods may work better for you than others. As highlighted in Chapter 2, what's critical is your attitude and that you have an open mind to challenging your paradigm and accepting new and different ideas. Remember, it's okay to be wrong! As Mark Manson says in *The Subtle Art of Not Giving a F*ck,* if you weren't wrong, then you wouldn't have any need to make changes to your life.

To begin, you'll need to set aside some time to intentionally think through the assumptions that you have about your concept and its obstacles.

While at first it might be difficult to be critically reflective, just like any skill, you will improve with practice.

Listed below are several tools you can use to assist you in starting to question your ideas. Pick one that makes sense to you and that you can easily apply to the problems you face in your everyday life. If you struggle to question your assumptions, grab a trusted buddy to do this with you who will call you out on your bullshit. The first place to start is by referring back to the list of obstacles you brainstormed above.

Cartesian doubt

One method of challenging assumptions is called Cartesian Doubt. The method was established by the 17th-century French philosopher René Descartes whose technique was to doubt every single fact until he could prove them to be true. When he applied it to his goal, which was the not-so-small question of how to know that things truly existed, he concluded, "I think; therefore I am."

When we apply this technique, we may not need to get so existential, but we can ask a similar question: How do I know this is true? Mark Manson suggests a similar technique by asking: "Is it possible that I am wrong?" By asking this question, you force yourself to consider the evidence for the obstacle that you've written down and thus consider whether it's actually true, only true under certain conditions, or perhaps that it's not true at all. You can do this by writing each obstacle in bold at the top of the page and then write your questions or supporting evidence beneath each one.

Let's consider an example. You're really dissatisfied with your current job. In fact, it genuinely sucks. You know you can't leave because financially you need an income and since the pandemic there are virtually no jobs going in your sector.

Now let's test your assumptions.

Let's first consider the statement that you're feeling dissatisfied with your current job. For starters, your problem could be reworded to read: "I am dissatisfied with *what I am doing* in my current job." It's most likely that there would be *some* things that you could do with your current employer that you would find satisfying. This statement then becomes a fact.

Likewise, it is a fact that you need a source of income to financially survive. Where you have made a major assumption is in saying, "you *can't* leave your job." There may be other means to derive an income other than from having a traditional office job. For instance, are there opportunities to consult or freelance in your area of expertise?

And have you *really* investigated whether there are "virtually no jobs" in your sector? Perhaps the pandemic has actually created demand for some specialized roles within your sector. You're also assuming that your sector is the only area in which you are employable. Even during the worst of COVID-19 lockdowns there were many areas of our economy that are actually booming – home shopping, online university courses, and so on.

As you can see, it's important to pull apart each piece of how you state your concept and to distinguish between facts and assumptions.

Socratic questioning
Socratic questioning is another technique by which you can challenge your assumptions. This involves asking the following questions:

- *Locate your assumption*: Why do I think this?
- *Challenge this assumption*: Is this always the case? How do I know this is true?
- *Look for objective evidence*: What evidence supports this idea? What evidence is against it?

- *Play the devil's advocate*: What might be another explanation or viewpoint of the situation?
- *Explore the implication and consequences*: What if I'm wrong? What are the consequences of my belief?
- *Distance yourself*: If a friend asked me for advice, what would I tell them?
- *Reflection*: What have I learned from this process?

Put these questions into a table and use it as a template that you can fill in for each obstacle.

Let's try applying this model to our example of the person who wants to improve the relationship with their partner. If we consider the first obstacle of not spending enough time together, we start by asking:

Why do I think this?

> I work long hours and so I come home late and leave early (this is just one possible explanation – in reality, there may often be multiple intertwined explanations – don't be afraid to write them all down.)

Next, challenge that assumption. Do you *have* to work long hours? What's the objective evidence to support this assumption?

- Is it an expectation at work?
- Will it lead to a bonus?
- Was I effective in doing what I had to do?
- Did I need to take all the breaks I took?
- Is there a need for more money?
- Do I need to stay at that job?
- Is there an option to work more flexible hours or work from home?

These are just some examples – you could ask many other questions at this point. It all depends on individual circumstances.

If it's true that you *do* have to work long hours, then a consequence may be that you have to change what you do outside of work hours to make the time you spend with your partner as being time that may enhance your relationship. Or perhaps you may be able to change your work hours so you can spend more time with your partner. And so on.

To assist in playing the devil's advocate, pretend you're a close friend, family member, or partner and consider what they would say. Or, perhaps go one step further and pretend that your friend is the one with the problem. What would you say to them? Or even better, skip the hypothetical and invite a close friend in to ask the hard questions.

Find the fundamental truths

Once you've applied one of the above techniques to challenge your assumptions, you should end up with a series of short fundamental truths or first principles from which you can build your creative solutions. The trick is to keep challenging your assumptions and breaking down your obstacles until you can't break it down any further without sounding silly or stretching the bounds of reality.

Looking at the previous example regarding the person who is dissatisfied with their job, their statement needed to be challenged. Ask the question: "Is it possible that I am wrong?" And the answer is most probably "yes." Now turn the statement around and ask: "Is there *anything* I could do at my current workplace that I would find satisfying?" In most cases, it would be very difficult to answer in the negative. If that's the case, then your concept needs to be reworded to state: "I am dissatisfied with what I am doing in my current job." By accurately stating your concept and wording it as a series of fundamental truths, you leave open the opportunity of identifying a far greater range of possible solutions.

It's hard to generate a set of first principles when you try it for the first time, but the more you practice and even the more time you spend thinking about it, the easier it gets. Remember, mistakes are an inevitable part of the creative process, so getting it wrong is to be expected and is not wrong. Go back to Step 1 or 2 and try again. Eventually, you will get there.

Step 2: Gather Raw Materials

Now you have the first principles from which to create new ideas and solutions AND you have the ingredients. So, how do you get the new ideas? See, the thing is, inspiration doesn't come without preparation. The biggest mistake people make is they assume that creativity comes naturally, so they wait for it to just hit them.

While creative ideas seem to be magical accidents that just appear, this is simply not true. In his book *A Technique for Producing Ideas*, James Young suggested that if you apply the right method and principles, anyone can produce creative solutions. He states that the ability to produce new combinations is dependent on the ability to see relationships between different facts. We've already done the work in Step 1 to produce the facts, now let's focus on how to see different relationships between them. To find different relationships between our first principles, we introduce new information to give us alternative perspectives. It's kind of like turning the end of a kaleidoscope to see different patterns.

The R in the C-R-E-A-T-E process is all about gathering **raw materials** relevant to the problem you're trying to solve or concept you're attempting to realize. These are the dots that you need to join. The more raw materials you gather, the more possible connections you'll see between your issues and the more likely you are to find a creative solution. And the more remote the connection or association between the facts is, the more the creative the solution.

The three Rs

The process of gathering raw materials can be summarized in the three Rs of creativity: research, reach out, and recall.

Research

The process of gathering raw materials usually starts with research. If you're a blogger, this may involve looking at other blogs that get lots of page views or tracking your analytics to see what content your audience is engaging with, how long their stay is on your site, and where/when they bounce. If you're a business, this may involve investigating relevant market insights or perhaps conducting surveys into customer experience and satisfaction. If you're dealing with personal issues, you could read different content about how to improve relationships or attend a personal development workshop. At this point you just want to be gathering information rather than trying to analyze or apply the information to your specific concept.

In his book *The Six Thinking Hats*, Edward de Bono lists a series of questions that each person can ask themselves when trying to determine what specific information they should be gathering:

- *What information do I have?*
- *What information do I need?*
- *What information is missing?*
- *What questions do I need to ask?*
- *How do I get the information I need?*

Back to our imaginary blogger. Perhaps they identify that they have information on the number of pageviews their blog gets but realize they don't have any statistics or information about what types of blog posts are most frequently read on other similar sites, and they don't know the most effective ways to advertise their blog. They might then do some further research to investigate how they can find that information, what research already exists, and how to access it.

Young emphasizes not to just gather raw materials related to your specific problem, but also to gather general material from all sorts of areas that may seem unrelated. He believes that new ideas come from a combination of general and specific knowledge. So, don't feel guilty for binging the latest Netflix documentary on American cults, or for spending the first five minutes of the workday browsing the pages of *The Guardian*. These can slowly feed the information base from which your brain can generate ideas. Continue to follow the references in Wikipedia pages and chase the rabbit holes on YouTube. If you only ever looked at knowledge specific to the existing problem, then it will be less likely that you come up with a creative and different solution to the problem. Think back to the chef analogy. If you only have a limited number of ingredients, the combinations that you can make are also going to be limited.

However, it's important to appreciate here that although an abundance of raw materials provides a greater number of potential combinations (or dots being joined) to form an element, creative ideas can come from whatever information you have at hand. As we'll see later, it's the creative thought excursions that ultimately determine whether or not the joining together of seemingly unrelated dots will occur. So, while collecting as many raw materials as you can is important, it's also important what you do with the information you have. Again, much like the chef analogy, some of the best and most creative recipes around the world come from populations in situations where they had to make do with very limited ingredients. Dishes like the South Korean Budae-jjigae, or Army base stew, arose following the Korean War when food was scarce, and people combined whatever US Army surplus foods they could scrounge or smuggle to create a delicious meal that is still much beloved in the country today.

Similarly, Dr. Seuss's *Green Eggs and Ham* serves as a great example of making the most out of limitations. In 1960, Dr. Seuss took on a bet with his publisher, Bennett Cerf, the co-founder of Random House, that he couldn't write a book with 50 or fewer distinct words. Bennett had based this challenge on the fact that Seuss's previous book, *The Cat in the Hat*, used only 223 words drawn from a list of 348 required words for beginner readers to learn. The agreed wager was $50. Fast forward to the present and 2020 marks the 60th year that the book has been in publication. The book has gone on to sell more than 60 million copies and has been adapted to stage and screen. Bennett was understandably quite happy to lose that bet and cough up the $50.

Collecting as many resources as you can is important. But as these examples show, it's what you *do* with the resources is what really matters. Sometimes, even a chef with a limitless pantry struggles to come up with creative new dishes.

Reach out

Part of the process of gathering raw materials must involve reaching out to other people. I've always been of the view that a good idea doesn't care who had it. Ultimately, it doesn't matter where the ideas originate; it matters where they take you. Reaching out may be to a mentor, people who have experienced similar issues as you, people who you find inspiring, a therapist or other professional, or maybe just a close friend or colleague. Tell them about the problem you're experiencing and the progress you've made in thinking through the problem. You may even want to share some of the ideas and insights you've had already. Reaching out to others is important because different people will bring new perspectives to the problem.

In her book *The Creator's Code*, Amy Wilkinson notes that respectful debate between individuals can spur further progress than when a person questions themselves. She attributes this to cognitive diversity, which means that different people think differently and bring varying perspectives to solving problems. Wilkinson quotes the research of Katherine Philips who found that by engaging with more diverse perspectives, individuals become more alert when considering that information and more open to rethinking their own perspectives and consequently, more likely to solve problems. Conversely, groups with people who thought similarly were less effective at solving problems as they became stuck in the same viewpoint.

One historical example of this is Bletchley Park, the center of the Allied operation to crack the Enigma code that the Germans used to send messages during World War II. The Allies gathered men and women from different countries and different backgrounds; linguists, military strategists, mathematicians, engineers, cryptographers, historians, philosophers, and even people who solved cryptic crosswords, whose different perspectives ultimately allowed them to crack the code and eventually win the war.

A contemporary example can be found in the way Google have designed their offices around the world. In contrast to traditional hierarchical office layouts with senior management on the upper floors and juniors on the lower floors, Google realized it's important for people of all levels to work together to create and share information. Google promoted an office culture called "casual collision," which results in the bringing together of employees from different parts of the organization that would have not likely otherwise met. The company purposely located each workspace to stimulate creativity and encourage social interaction with members from structurally separate teams. For instance, in Google's New York headquarters, no part of the office is more than 150 feet from food. Whether it's a restaurant, coffee lounge, or cafeteria, employees are encouraged to snack more, chat more and, most importantly, create more. Google understands that collaboration between people from different backgrounds and perspectives promotes creativity and drives production.

But there is a trade-off between comfort and effectiveness. The downside to cognitive diversity is that we tend to feel more uncomfortable with people who think differently, and this is a barrier that we must try and overcome. Being uncomfortable is an impediment to creative thinking, as we saw in Chapter 1, and we should all try to become more comfortable with change.

The take-home message from this is that while it may be tempting to only reach out to people who you admire or who you're familiar with, you're more likely to find new raw materials and creative ideas by speaking to people who are different to you. I encourage you to be bold and seek out new and challenging perspectives even if (at first) it makes you feel uncomfortable. Reaching out and socializing outside your normal circle of friends brings new perspectives to the concept you're working on. Take advantage of all those LinkedIn connections and start some exciting conversations. New people don't know all your thought patterns and old stories, so you'll have to revisit your existing inner monologues. The refreshing perspectives will help to surface new thinking and possibly the formation of some creative elements to help develop your concept. Sometimes reaching out to others can even prompt collaboration as others also become excited about your concept. Collaboration and creativity go hand-in-hand – so go ahead and embrace any offers to collaborate. You may achieve even more than the concept you first came up with.

Even if the person doesn't give any new perspective or ideas, reaching out is still extremely valuable because the process of articulating your thoughts helps you clarify the issues. Maybe you've experienced the opposite effect – when you are trying to explain to a friend a really funny video that you watched, or trying to explain something new you learned at a conference, but then you seem to get a bit confused and miss the punchline or main point, and your friend doesn't really get it. In your scenario, as you reach out to others and they ask you further clarifying questions to understand your assumptions, the issues, and your concept, this will help you identify whether you clearly understand those things because you're forced to articulate them. And when you get stuck or confused, this tells you that this is the area you need to gather more raw materials for or that you may need to rethink your concept or further question your assumptions to generate creative ideas for your concept.

Recall

If you're anything like me, you probably forget things a lot and frequently start your sentences with "I can't remember where I heard this, but..." When you gather your raw materials, Young emphasizes that you need to record the sources of your raw materials. This can sound like a lot of effort, but it doesn't have to be. It can be as simple as typing a thought in the Notes app on your phone and pasting the link to the post that you were reading that inspired the thought or saving interesting articles or comments you read on social media to look at later. Or if you're a bit old fashioned like me, write in in a notebook or on post-it notes. Austin Kleon calls it a "swipe file," either a digital or analog one where you take pictures of or paste in records, items you find inspiring or stuff you want to steal. A journal is great for recording thoughts, feelings, and those little snippets of information as and when they arise. It's also is a great way to structure and develop ideation habits. If you don't keep a journal already, start one today.

Recording snippets of information is important for two reasons. First, the actual process of writing down a thought or deliberately bookmarking a page helps embed something in your memory. Your brain is forced to process information in a more detailed way, which means the information is more likely to be retained. And if the information isn't stored in your brain, then it can't be used to produce those creative ideas. If it's not there, it can't be recalled. Mlodinow suggests that every day we are exposed to the equivalent information of the contents of a 300-page book. But with so much information available every day, it's no surprise that unless we purposely store information, it falls straight back out of our head and is forgotten.

The second reason why recording the information is important is for those moments where you think to yourself, "Now where did I get that from…" When you get your ideas, you want to be able to recall your sources so that you can re-examine them and further develop those ideas.

It's truly amazing how much information is stored in our brain. In 2016, neuroscientists at the Salk Institute in California came up with new estimates for the human brain's memory capacity to be 10-fold more than previously thought. Researchers also discovered that, unlike a computer that codes information as zeros and ones, a brain cell uses 26 different ways to code its "bits." They calculated that the brain could store one petabyte (or a quadrillion bytes) of information. That's more information than is contained on the entire internet! But there is a small catch, the overwhelming majority of this information is irretrievable. So, when you need to remember a phone number, a shopping list, or a set of instructions, you rely on what psychologists and neuroscientists refer to as working memory. It's the ability to hold and manipulate information in mind over brief intervals. It's for things that are important to you in the present moment, but not 10 or 20 years from now. Capacity of our working memory is limited – we can keep only a certain amount of information "in mind" at any one time.

On the other hand, long-term memory is characterized by a much larger storage capacity. The information it holds is also more durable and stable. Neuroscientists have long regarded working memory as a gateway into long-term storage. If we can retrieve information from the long-term memory into our working memory, then that information can become more permanent and more readily available to solve problems and create new ideas. This is where our five senses come into play. By way of sensory association, the stimulation of a particular sensory perception can revive associated memories and even emotions of a previous experience. For instance, a special song that, when you hear it, takes you back to a certain place and time. We see that when our subconscious is at play – perhaps when we're daydreaming, or asleep, or engaged in thought excursions, then information stored in our long-term memory can come to the surface. By tapping into this huge reservoir of information, we can increase our chances of coming up with new ideas or more creative solutions to problems.

In the writing of this book, I got snippets of information from a myriad of sources: articles from in-flight magazines, billposter slogans, TV commercials, random conversations, and even blackboard "message of the day" outside cafes and stores. It doesn't matter where these bits of information come from; the important thing is to store them somewhere so they can be recalled. As soon as you recall something in your mind, write it down because that piece of information can very easily vanish. I find that much of my recalling comes to me around 3:30 in the morning, so I always keep my notebook on my bedside table. The real challenge in recalling information is the ability to recall the information you need when you need it.

Step 3: Form the Elements

Ideas are a bit like ninjas: after all this work searching for it, it's only until after you've stopped looking, when you least expect it, that an idea or solution will creep up on you. It happens when two bits of information come together – when two of the dots are jointed – that produces a good idea. Now we've created an **element**. This is the first E in the C-R-E-A-T-E process. You've formed an element that relates to your concept in some way. Just as in nature, the base elements are the building blocks for compounds, so too are creative elements – they're the building blocks for your concept. We can equate the formation of an element to an "a-ha" moment when the proverbial light bulb switches on.

However, this is far from the end of the process. When you look at your new idea for a second time, it often doesn't seem quite so marvelous and shiny as it did when you first thought of it. It may even have some fairly large gaps or seem unrealistic. And so, the process continues, and your concept progressively develops with the addition or removal of elements formed by the joining together of dots. This may involve going back to some of the processes in Step 2 to further refine the idea or perhaps even going back to the beginning of the process to refine your concept. This is why the C-R-E part of the C-R-E-A-T-E process is known as the Creative Triad because you cycle around these three components continuing to create elements that will gradually develop your concept.

There are, however, certain conditions that are conducive to the creation of elements. In the next chapter, we'll see the importance of creating the right atmosphere to enable you to freely explore your thought excursions. But more on that later.

Barriers to Upholding Our Concepts

Now that we have seen how developing a concept – one that is *really* important to us – provides both the goal and motivation to realize our aspirations, the art of creating appears to be relatively straightforward provided we follow the process. So then if we all have the ability to practice how to become creative, how come we aren't all practicing creatives? There may be a relatively simple answer. There are two significant impediments to creativity:

1. The fear of change and the risk of failure that change may bring
2. The fear of being wrong and being rejected by others as a result.

One of the things we fear the most is change. Humans have an inbuilt aversion to certain types of change, particularly *intra*-personal change that we discussed earlier in the book. We naturally assume that the risks of change are greater than the risks of not changing even if the risks of staying the same are, in reality, more likely or more serious. Why is this? Well, to put it simply, it's because change is hard. I'm sure at some point while reading this book, you thought, "who the hell has time for all this?" This process isn't easy, and it does take time and effort. I won't lie; doing things the same way you've always done will always be easier. The selling point of this process isn't that it's easy – it's that it produces results. Success doesn't happen to people by accident; it's the product of planning and purpose-driven action. Hard work is a necessary corollary.

We fear change because we consider the equation: change = risk of failure. This is perfectly natural. Historically, fears have played an important role in keeping human beings alive. The fear that something might be in the cave stopped our distant ancestors from sleeping in caves and encountering hungry bears. Being cautious was seen as wise, encapsulated in the classic idiom, "curiosity killed the cat." The reality is that because this mode of thinking is only used for big important concepts, it means the stakes are high. In a post-COVID economy, businesses are in a more precarious environment than ever. Trying something new could mean the end of the business. Equally, for concepts in the personal realm, failure can result in the breakdown of relationships or a decline in mental or physical health. The fear of failure is well justified. So how do we overcome these fears?

The solution to overwhelming fear is to come back to your concept – the thing that drives you. Is it worth the risk? Is it worth the risk of failure if it may mean saving your marriage or living a happier, more fulfilled life? While a new business strategy might risk failure, is a slow decline by doing the same old thing any better? This is why identifying your concept is so important. If you don't believe in your concept, if you don't *really* want it, then when the process is too hard or the change will seem too big, you'll find yourself procrastinating from doing the hard work or worse, you'll just give up entirely. Elon Musk admitted he's scared of failure too. SpaceX and Tesla both almost collapsed at the same time in 2008 and again in 2013. However, his advice is exactly the same: "If something is important enough or you believe that something is important enough, even if you are scared, you still keep going."

The good news is that once you know about your tendencies to avoid change and a fear of failure, you'll be more likely to attempt to keep an objective perspective while making these decisions. Another top tip to help maintain objectivity and not allow your fears to overwhelm you is to reach out. Other people are more removed and, therefore, more likely to call you out on your bullshit and help you get on with the job.

Our fear of being wrong is closely related to our fear of failure, except it's driven more by our perception that others will think we're incompetent. However, looking at some of the world's most famous people, they always seem to be outsiders who ignore the opinions and expectations of others. Look at these quotes from some successful creatives:

> *"Don't think about making art; just get it done. Let everyone else decide if it's good or bad, whether they love it or hate it. While they are deciding, make even more art."* Andy Warhol, American artist known for creating pop art.

> *"All great deeds and all great thoughts have a ridiculous beginning."* Albert Camus, French Nobel Prize-winning author and philosopher.

> *"Great things are not accomplished by those who yield to trends and fads and popular opinion."* Jack Kerouac, American poet and pioneer of the Beat generation.

> *"It is better to have enough ideas for some of them to be wrong than to be always right by having no ideas at all."* Edward de Bono, British psychologist and author who coined the term "lateral thinking."

"Do not fear to be eccentric in opinion, for every opinion now accepted was once eccentric." Bertrand Russell, British Nobel laureate and one of the founders of analytic philosophy.

What all of these quotes are getting at is that if you want success then that necessarily comes with a) being wrong, and b) others thinking that you're getting it wrong (even when you're getting it right). This is especially the case when you're trying to be creative because you're looking for a solution that doesn't yet exist. If you wanted to avoid being wrong then you could just copy the solutions that are already out there, that already work. But true creativity requires being a little bit wacky. These quotes demonstrate that what drives the creative to endure the critique of others and your failures is that creators *truly* believe in the work they're doing. Developing their concept is more important than being accepted. Could you say the same about your concept?

This belief in your concept can be hardest when you reach out to others and they question or criticize not only your thinking process but sometimes even the concept itself. Criticism or even just feedback can be really hard to bear if the problem is something that you're really invested in and can be especially difficult to hear when the comments are accurate, and you have to admit that perhaps you were wrong. However, feedback can be incredibly important to further develop your concepts and ideas so you can succeed. In a 2012 interview with Kevin Rose, Elon Musk spoke of the importance of feedback:

> ▮▮ *"I'm a huge believer in taking feedback. I'm trying to create a mental model that's accurate, and if I have a wrong view on something, or if there's a nuanced improvement that can be made, I'll say, 'I used to think this one thing that turned out to be wrong—now thank goodness I don't have that wrong belief.'"*

One of the most significant creators and inventors in American history was Thomas Edison. He is perhaps best known for inventing the first long-lasting, commercially practical incandescent light bulb. He was the father of many other breakthroughs, including the first phonograph and the motion picture camera, and he was influential in developing the first economically viable way of distributing light, heat, and power from a central station. But it was when he was developing the electric light bulb and even after 1,000 failed prototypes, he *knew* he could create it. In the spirit of a true creator, he said, "At least I now know a thousand ways it won't work," and continued his endeavors.

Keeping in mind the importance of your concept's success can help you take on the critique of others. While it can be hard to hear your ideas and choices being questioned, it will always be harder, in the long run, to not succeed at whatever your concept might be. The uncomfortable awkwardness is worth it.

The cognitive process of creating

After the initial period of intense concentration in reviewing all the raw material you've gathered, and having explored relationships between the bits of information, you may find that your creative ideas do not magically appear. There may be foreshadowing of ideas that in some way relate to your concept, but the formation of elements – the "ah-ha" moments – may still appear to be rather elusive. As you continue to cycle the Creative Triad you will reach a stage when you run out of potential combinations but still with no clear insight to a solution. At this stage you'll have exhausted all your mental energy so now it's time to walk away and put the concept and everything else out of your mind as completely as you can. Even keeping in mind something as trivial as what you are going to have for dinner can impede your 20-20 Thinking. This is when you hand over to your subconscious to continue the heavy creative lifting.

To those around you, when you move into this relaxed state of mind, it may appear that you're procrastinating or engaging in mindless day-dreaming. For many people, this has negative connotations. But, as Leonard Mlodinow states in his book *Elastic*, "research shows a positive correlation between procrastination and creativity, because putting off conscious attempts to solve problems and make decisions, we provide ourselves more time to fit in those episodes of unconscious consideration." This is when we're in the best position, in terms of mindset, to engage in thought excursions.

With recent advances in neuroscience, researchers have identified a particular region of the brain known as the 'association cortices' that is responsible for where our thinking takes place when we're not consciously thinking. Located within these cortices are our association neurons which are the source of our inventiveness and what allow us to think of new ideas rather than merely react. Scientifically, this accounts for why, when we are daydreaming and allowing our mind to wander, that we can come up with new ideas and solve problems when our conscious efforts to do so had failed. As weird as it may sound, when our minds are at rest, what's really happening is that thoughts are bouncing back and forth, or if we relate it to our Creative Triad process, when all our bits of information are being continually cycled. So that's why when you are doing something mindless, like mowing your lawns or lying awake at 3:30 in the morning, your mind is in a state when it is most free to wander.

The reason for introducing the Creative Monk model of creativity is that in having been structured on imaginary impossibilities, it actually primes our mind to move toward its relaxed default mode of thought and thereby enables it to harness the full creative potential of our unconscious mind.

This now brings us to a part of the C-R-E-A-T-E process that can best be described as a continuation of the Creative Triad cycle. The BIG difference is that the process now takes place entirely in our subconscious mind. In the previous chapter, I introduced the concept of thought excursions. Thought excursions are explorations into that which is creatively possible but usually way beyond the extremities of what you know and the paradigms you keep. Although developing our concept and gathering raw materials occurred within the realm of our consciousness, thought excursions happen at the subconscious level and are what enables the formation of elements by bringing together remotely associated connections. The difficulty in gaining an understanding of how this cognitively happens is related to the fact that our subconscious doesn't follow rules of logic nor conform to rational reasoning. The thinking that happens in our subconscious mind is the most creative precisely *because* it's free from these impediments that restrict our creative imagination.

Earlier, I mentioned how children are such incredibly creative thinkers. They imagine without any of the limitations that we, as adults, place on our thinking. Children are divergent thinkers capable of producing a range of ideas — freely, generously, and without any fear of peer pressures. Children are not constrained by thinking only what society says is possible as they see no reason why they can't make the impossible a reality. As adults, we lose the innocence of our childhood imagination. So, to assist you in visualizing what the continuation of the Creative Triad cycle in the subconscious looks like, I've created a model that illustrates the subconscious thinking process and how connections are made between disparate bits of information.

We discussed in the previous chapter that the fundamental difficulty in constructing such a model of creativity is because the overwhelming majority of our creative ideas develop in our subconscious mind and so, by definition, it's not possible for us to consciously know what's going on in there. With the model I've developed that borrows significantly from recent neuroscientific research, we're able to visualize the "mechanics" of how the subconscious process of creating ideas operates. But first, we need to convince ourselves that exploring the impossible is not a futile, childish undertaking.

> "There is no use trying," said Alice. "One can't believe impossible things."
>
> "I daresay you haven't had much practice," said the Queen.
>
> "When I was your age, I always did it for half an hour a day. Why, sometimes I've believed as many as six impossible things before breakfast."

The above extract from *Alice's Adventures in Wonderland* was part of Lewis Carroll's journey into the subconscious. But there is more to "believing the impossible" than what we may have thought. Alison Gopnik is an American Professor of Psychology at the University of California. She attained her doctorate in the field of experimental psychology from Oxford University In 1980. In her book, *The Philosophical Baby*, Gopnik explores how young children cognitively develop by using processes similar to those explored by neuroscientists, including experimenting on their environment. Gopnik explains how an environment maximized for an infant's cognitive development is one that is safe to explore. Through extensive psychological studies she has found, that children who play pretend and practice "believing the impossible" tend to develop more advanced cognition. "A lot of what they do in pretend play is take a hypothesis and follow it out to the logical conclusion," says Gopnik. They are better at understanding hypothetical thinking and they tend to develop a more advanced ability to connect remotely associated elements.

Now with the scientific evidence behind us it's now time to "look and see" what's happening in our subconscious mind. Believing the impossible can assist in training our inner-selves, and to acquire the habits, that enable us to think beyond the realms of our everyday lives.

An Imaginary Interlude

Before we go into the detail of the workings of the Creative Monk Model in the next section, I'm sure there are a few readers who still have reservations as to how something imaginary and considered impossible can provide any value to what we do and how we think in the real world. I'm sure that Alice had much the same misgivings when she ventured down the rabbit hole.

To illustrate the point that imagining the impossible *is* possible and that it can be done to produce something of value, I draw upon another math-related concept. At some stage in our schooling we've all had to learn math, whether it was in kindergarten when we counted aloud on our fingers, or later at high school when we ventured into the world of geometry and other more complex topics. Yet, whichever area of math we studied, we could always find – if we were so motivated to inquire – a practical reason and application in the real world. Being able to count allowed us to check that we weren't being ripped off when we bought candy at the store and simple geometric calculations ensured we put the correct amount of Prosecco into our Aperol Spritz. Both very important life-skills. But what could be less practical than a number described as imaginary? However, if it weren't for imaginary numbers, we would have no quantum theory and, hence, no electronics – and so, the contemporary world as we know it would simply not exist. Even if the concept of imaginary numbers still feels a bit strange and mysterious, be reassured you're in good company, because many of the most brilliant minds over the centuries have also struggled in comprehending this ground-breaking idea.

When majoring in pure mathematics in my undergraduate science degree, I studied a branch of math known as imaginary numbers. You may recall from high school that in the rules of math, two negative numbers multiplied together must always make a positive number, hence -4 x -4 = +16, and so on. According to the traditional rules of math, the square root of a negative number can't exist, so asking someone what is the square root of -1 would be like saying, "You have a bowl of rice and a bag of potatoes. How do you make chicken kiev?" Before the introduction of this new set of numbers, mathematicians considered solving problems such as $\sqrt{-16}$ impossible. However, over time, some mathematicians worked out that they *could* create such a number to solve these equations, so they created the number $\sqrt{-1}$ (more commonly known as i), due to the fact that people simply needed it.

It was the 16th century Italian mathematician and engineer, Rafael Bombelli, who, through a process of visualization, first came up with the concept of imaginary numbers, but it would be another 300 years until mathematicians would finally prove his theorem. And what's even more amazing is that these previously – believed to be "impossible" – numbers were able to integrate with the traditional *real* numbers to form *complex* numbers. Bombelli imagined the possibility of a series of numbers as being in a "parallel" system – akin to an additional dimension from the tradition system of math which we're familiar with. The reason why it took centuries for others to accept this new series of numbers is that they had no reference within their existing dimensions of mathematics – that is their "mathematical" paradigms – to even be able to visualize what the extra dimension of imaginary numbers could look like. This would be like asking a person living in a two-dimensional world to explain to an inhabitant of a three-dimensional world, what a shadow was. But once Rafael had convinced himself that such a series *could* exist, he methodically, in a step-by-step process, explained in his 1579 publication *L'algebra*, how they could co-exist in the world of mathematics.

When I describe in some detail the mechanics of the Creative Monk Model in the next section, you'll see direct parallels between the ability to visualize our own subconscious though processes and what Bombelli has done in introducing a new dimension in mathematics to explain his imaginary system of numbers. Both Bombelli's model and our Creative Monk Model allow you to imagine something within an existing system or framework that appears an impossibility, but once imagined, provides for the realization of preconceived concepts to achieve specific goals.

So how did mathematicians create, let alone conceive of the idea that 'i' may have useful purposes? To explain this, we should realize that math itself is an invention. Math is *not* a science. It doesn't represent reality, nor for that matter, does it even attempt to. It's a system that merely works. Like most systems, it was designed for a specific purpose, just as I have developed a system for creating creativity with a particular reason in mind. The rules relating to complex numbers are no different than the rules relating to any other branch of math. The discomfort you feel is the awkwardness not between reality and the i series but between the (deceptively named) 'real' series and its imaginary counterpart.

Imaginary numbers seem to run against common sense on a basic level, but if you accept them as a *system*, then they make sense. Nothing makes two plus two equal four any more correct than me telling you that my dog is named Teddy. So, two plus two only really equals four because we're told it is so. If we want to play a game, we must agree to be bound by the rules of the game. So too with imaginary numbers.

What I love most about imaginary numbers is that it took centuries for us to understand and accept the paradigm shift required to accept the concept, but in the end, we reaped the spoils. But because mathematicians kept working towards understanding something purely theoretical at the time, we now have the tools pivotal to modern fields like electrical engineering and quantum mechanics. Ask any physical scientist or engineer how they would get by without using the square root of minus one. Civil engineers use i to study stresses on beams and to study resonance. Complex numbers assist mechanical and aeronautical engineers to study the flow of fluid around objects, such as water around a pipe or air passing over an airfoil. We wouldn't have access to accurate weather forecasts if not for imaginary numbers. Without using imaginary numbers to calculate circuit theories, you would not be able to read this on your smart device.

This rather lengthy example serves to illustrate – albeit within a pure mathematical context – a rather simple yet most important point; that

In summary, the overarching objective of presenting this example of imaginary numbers is that it serves as a pragmatic precursor to presenting the Creative Monk Model. We have seen that through the process of visualizing, then creating, a seemingly impossible concept, can derive a practical and useful outcome in the real world.

The Creative Monk Model

We need to train our mind to think in pictures so we can better understand the various steps of the creative process. The task, therefore, is to create our own intra-personal laboratory where we can conduct thought excursions. As thought excursions are a highly personal journey, the last thing you want to do is draw attention to what you're doing. To avoid this, John Cleese suggests that we need to create our own personal space-time oasis. To get the most out of the process, we need to conduct our thought excursions in an atmosphere that's free from the pressures of everyday life and the clutches of disruptive technologies. This provides us the requisite freedom in both the spatial and temporal dimensions.

In terms of 20-20 Thinking and the C-R-E-A-T-E process, consider all the bits of information that you have gathered in the raw materials phase that are continually cycling around in the C-R-E circle. Now study Escher's 1960 etching masterpiece *Ascending and Descending* that is reproduced below. Let's now try, as Einstein suggests, "think in pictures."

Figure 11: Escher – Ascending and Descending

Focus intensely on the two files of monks trudging forever upwards and infinitely downwards on this eternal staircase. Now overlay in your mind the Creative Triad process of concept, raw materials, and elements. Consider each of these monks as the carriers of all these bits of information – some ascending and some descending, but all continually moving. Now imagine that this is what's happening in your subconscious mind. All these bits of information are simultaneously cycling, in opposing directions, and as each monk passes the other, the opportunity arises for a relationship to be established between two pieces of disparate information. It's only when two bits of information form an association that an element is formed, and the dots are joined. Accordingly, when an element is formed it will either broaden (ascending monks) your concept or narrow (descending monks) your concept.

If you *are* able to visualize this model, I really believe it will assist you in understanding how thought excursions function within your sub-conscious. Your mind naturally wanders, but instead of seeing this as a tangential distraction, just let it wander. Better still, by encouraging your mind to travel to the outer edge of what's normal, you can turn a daydream into a productive brainstorm. This first requires the conscious realization that everything you know about the world and how you relate within it has been shaped for you by paradigms. The paradigm shift of the COVID-19 pandemic has destabilized our epoch, and our paradigms are left without precedent. Precedent of the past has created our models of the everyday – of monotonous, conforming routine. Now, you're tasked with creating your own new models.

Now, more than ever, you have the power to individualize it and manifest for yourself your own path. To achieve this, we must train ourselves to think beyond the realms of the thinkable, the plausible, and the possible. We must embark upon a flight to a land of possibilities: to a land in which the seemingly impossible become plausible realities. By adopting this model of creativity, we are now better positioned to participate in thought excursions.

Application to the Real World

Now that we've explored the subconscious workings of the creative process and the advantages of engaging in thought excursions as part of our 20-20 Thinking, you may be asking: but does it really work? Let's look at some historical examples of where the creative process and the use of first principles thinking has worked successfully as well as how businesses have used this kind of thinking to survive the COVID-19 crisis.

Innovation throughout history

It's pretty hard to visit IKEA without buying at least something. Just about everyone has at least one item in their home from IKEA. For young people living out of home for the first time, shops like IKEA are an absolute lifesaver with their cheap yet good-quality furniture and household items. One advantage of buying from IKEA is their flat-packed furniture. It means you can walk into a store and take home what you buy there and then rather than having to pay more and wait days or weeks for it to arrive.

As the story goes, flat-packed furniture was invented in 1956 when an IKEA worker took the legs off one of their tables to fit it inside the delivery van. This led the company to challenge the assumption that furniture could only be sold in one piece. Thinking function over form and using first principles, IKEA identified that while the concept or end result was how to get a piece of furniture in a consumer's house, this didn't necessarily require the furniture to be transported in that form. In fact, delivering furniture in one piece had a lot of problems: it was bulky, more expensive and time-consuming, and items often got damaged and needed to be returned. These issues ultimately added to the cost of supplying the product. Until that point, people assumed that this was the best, and indeed only, way to supply furniture. And although there were likely many delivery drivers who had taken legs off tables to fit in their vans, it only took one company to pay attention, to listen, and to then research different ideas to land on their flat-packed furniture solution.

Many furniture companies have since copied the idea to manufacture and sell similar flat-packed products. IKEA remains one of the most successful retail companies today, and this is largely because they continue to innovate. Recently IKEA added an augmented reality feature to their catalog that allows users to visualize what products would look like in their homes. They've also begun making furniture from recycled materials and introduced a smart home lighting system. It's clear that creative thinking is an integral part of IKEA's ongoing business strategy.

With the COVID-19 crisis forcing more people to spend time indoors, the number of subscribers to platforms like Netflix have skyrocketed. In 2020, Netflix had 182.8 million subscribers, which is more than the population of the UK, France, Portugal, The Netherlands, Belgium, Finland, and Ireland *combined*. This sizeable base generated $20.2 billion in revenue for the streaming service. These are the kind of statistics that every business dreams of accruing. Netflix began as a DVD subscription service back in 1997 and were an online rival to video rental stores like Blockbuster. Subscribers would pay a fee to have DVDs delivered in the mail that either they selected or that their algorithm calculated as a popular choice. What made Netflix really grow in size was when they switched from mailing DVDs to providing online video on demand. Within three years of Netflix switching to a streaming-based platform, Blockbuster went into liquidation.

These two consumer video providers had the same concept: to provide customers with access to vast libraries of movies to watch at home without the cost of purchasing them outright. However, one became far more successful than the other. While Blockbuster continued with the model that had always worked, assuming it was the best option, Netflix was examining the latest advances in technology to determine how to combine this new tech with movies to provide the concept in the most attractive ways to consumers. This just goes to show that even when business is going well, in order to continue stimulating growth, leaders need to constantly re-evaluate their concept and explore recombining elements to give customers better options. They need to prioritize the function that their concept serves over the form that their concept takes.

The Netflix example also reveals the importance of utilizing technology to generate creative solutions. New technology is often a disruptor to society's "normal." A strong concept needs to embrace this disruption. Netflix is also a demonstration of the distinction made earlier in the chapter between chefs and cooks. Following the success of Netflix, we've seen a slew of streaming services such as Amazon Prime, Hulu, Disney+, as well as most traditional commercial television and cable networks joining the pack as they attempt to compete in an increasingly saturated market. While these other services have largely been successful, that success is limited because their profits derive from copying someone else's good idea rather than innovating ahead of the market.

Innovation amid the COVID-19 pandemic

Looking more closely at the present, we can already see how COVID-19 has become a corona event for many businesses. The pandemic has forced them to think more creatively and utilize 20-20 Thinking principles to continue to stay in business. While it may seem counter-intuitive, evidence suggests that the highest rates of entrepreneurship occur alongside high unemployment during times of economic downturn. Companies like Airbnb, Dropbox, and Uber all emerged from the global financial crisis in 2007-8. While the coronavirus is a clear stressor for many businesses, there's also lots of evidence to suggest that significant entrepreneurship is already going on.

Many businesses are repurposing existing equipment to fulfill increased demands sparked by the pandemic. Throughout the world, distilleries have used equipment normally used to create gin and other alcohols, and companies have redirected its output to create hand sanitizer. The clear concept that they were working with was to keep business going, so they challenged the assumption that the only business they could do was produce alcohol for consumption. Instead, they examined consumer demand and their own capabilities and identified a different crossover – alcohol as a disinfectant.

Other industries have also made similar adaptations. Car manufacturers like Toyota and Ford have been producing PPE gear for health workers and participated in the VentilatorChallengeUK, where various manufacturers designed and produced ventilator machines to be used by the UK's

National Health Service. The website covidinnovations.com contains a list of many ways that businesses have innovated in response to the pandemic – check it out if you are looking for enterprising inspiration.

The forced lockdowns during some of the worst times of the pandemic has had a massive impact on the entertainment and hospitality industries, and both have had to radically rethink the concept of providing food and entertainment to customers. This is especially the case for fine dining restaurants who have had to compete with cheaper takeout restaurants who were already using online delivery platforms like UberEats and DoorDash for some time. Different restaurants took different approaches. Some created hampers with gourmet meals and matching wines designed specifically to be eaten at home. Others provided ingredients for some of their classic dishes and included detailed tutorials on how to cook the dish at home – some even came with a curated Spotify playlist to be played while cooking. Some bars have done to-go cocktails in cute little bottles while others have DIY cocktail hampers. A Sydney-based bar, Gin Lane, created a monthly subscription option where users could subscribe to receive boutique gin from different craft distillers each month. Many cafes have taken to offering grocery boxes to regular customers that contain a mix of pantry staples as well as signature ingredients that the cafe would normally use for certain dishes, allowing the cafe to support their suppliers and customers while still making a profit.

Cafes and restaurants used creativity to rethink their concept of how to deliver food to their customers based on first principles: their ingredients, location, staff, and existing customer base. I think the sheer number of ways in which different restaurants have innovated really demonstrates how the one concept of giving food to another person can be done in so many different ways, despite the usual image we have when we think of what it means to be a restaurant. This demonstrates that the creative solutions to concepts are endless, and there are always more alternatives to find. This is what the C-R-E-A-T-E process is all about. Finding the key concept. Questioning your assumptions about that concept. Collecting raw materials. Joining dots to create elements to achieve that concept in a different way. There is no one right answer with creativity. That's both its beauty and its challenge.

While COVID-19 has forced many businesses to innovate to survive under the conditions of a pandemic, many of the creative solutions will have an ongoing effect on the way people do business in the future. How many more workplaces may be open to flexible working options now that they have been forced to make working from home an option for everyone? This can benefit many people who require flexible options, those who live further away, or those with other roles as parents or carers. When commercial airlines eventually resume regular service, their biggest competitor may well be Zoom, Microsoft Teams, or Skype rather than competing carriers.

The pandemic has also led to increased use of technology and digitization in entirely new areas of application. With a variety of online video conferencing platforms throughout the world, there have been virtual sessions of Parliament, doctors conducting virtual consultations with patients, virtual lectures and classes for domestic and international students continuing their studies while excluded from campus, and virtual hearings in tribunals and courts in the various jurisdictions. And whilst corporate video conferencing has been around for ages, it's only been during the COVID-19 restrictions on travel that it has *had* to be used. The delineation between discretionary and essential corporate travel in the future will most likely be redefined considering the cost of travel and the proven success of these communication platforms. Many of these developments, while induced or increased by the pandemic, will likely be carried forward into the next normal.

Perhaps the COVID-19 crisis will facilitate the development of creative solutions to some of the other big issues we face too. Time will tell which of these will stick and which will develop further into new innovations in the post-pandemic world.

Ultimately, while your corona event may only be temporary, the ideas that you generate and implement as a result of facing your corona dilemma can last and could have a long-term impact if you allow it to do so. The creative process is transformative and is always worth investing in.

The Journey Begins with the Concept

Let's take it back to the personal. Back to you. It's worth reiterating here that while the people we've discussed and quoted in this chapter may seem like extraordinary people who were "destined" to be creative, the truth is that creative thinking is just a process. You don't have to be special or born creative to use these models and processes because anyone and everyone can apply these ideas to the problems we all face.

I encourage you now to take a moment and think about your concept, the thing you want to achieve, the vision you have for your life. You *can* achieve this. It may be hard, and the solution may not come quickly, but it *is* possible. This chapter gives you the tools to start the process and find creative solutions. But if you want to fully understand how to get those creative ideas, then you'll need to delve into the subconscious, which I cover in the next chapter. All of this thinking, asking the hard questions, searching for ideas – they're all necessary, but on their own, they're not sufficient to properly generate creative ideas. After all, you can't force a creative idea. Otherwise, we would already be coming up with all sorts of creative ideas – and you wouldn't be reading this book.

Learnings from Chapter 4:

Creativity isn't a gift you have; it's a habit you can practice. However, you need to set aside time and energy into intentionally engaging with the creative process. The cycle of creative thinking is continuous – you just need to keep feeding your mind with information to enhance the likelihood of dots being joined. You must have the faith of your conviction and not be discouraged by what other people think. Then you will be able to generate creative ideas to achieve your concept.

Now go to **Chapter 6 – Habits** and relate the above learnings to the following habits:

- Habit #7 Are you unconcerned of what other people think about what you do?
- Habit #8 Do you have a mind that rarely slows down?

5

MAKING IDEAS HAPPEN

"Be less curious about people and more curious about ideas."

Marie Curie

In 1991, computer programmer Tom Baccei and his artist friend, Cheri Smith, created the first formatted color picture that could be viewed as a three-dimensional image with the naked eye. Their invention is described as a color random-dot auto-stereogram which they marketed as the *Magic Eye*. Stereograms were nothing new having been developed in the late 1950s by Béla Juresz, a neuroscientist. What was novel about what Tom and Cheri did was that they created the first stereogram as a single picture rather than having to view two pictures simultaneously.

Almost overnight their innovation sparked a worldwide 3D craze that became all the rage in the '90s. Their 32-page book, *Magic Eye: A New Way of Looking at the World* was released in 1993 and, together with its two sequels, appeared on the *New York Times* Best Seller list for a combined 73 weeks and sold more than 20 million copies. In Germany alone it became the number-one best-selling book of all time. With their technique patented, the creators went on the reap the rewards of their creativity.

Well, that's all very good news for Tom and Cheri, but what's that got to do with this book and with 20-20 Thinking? The short answer: A lot. You may be surprised to discover some rather uncanny parallels between the perceptive challenges involved in seeing 3D images and the cognitive processes required to engage in 20-20 Thinking. Let me explain.

The initial problem that Tom and Cheri encountered when launching their creation was that for most people, when presented with the *Magic Eye* pictures, all they could see was a series of repeated geometric images; where was the so-called 3D image? In fact, somewhere in the order of 50 per cent of people say they can never see the hidden images. So, what gives? Is there something wrong with these people's eyes? Are there really hidden pictures or is this all a hoax? Most difficulties in viewing the *Magic Eye* images have to do with the way the eyes work with each other and with the brain. To view 3D stereo images, both eyes have to work together as a coordinated team. If they're not pulling together, you're going to have some glitches in your binocular (two-eyed) vision or stereo vision – where the two slightly different views from your eyes are combined in the brain. This is known as binocular and stereo vision impairment. But these physiological impairments only account for a very small proportion of those people who are unable to see the 3D images. For those of us that *can* see these images, we discovered that depth is not perceived in the eye itself, but rather in the brain. To see the images, we need to train our *brain*.

Now, see if you can view the embedded 3D image below. (Hint: it has to do with aviation!)

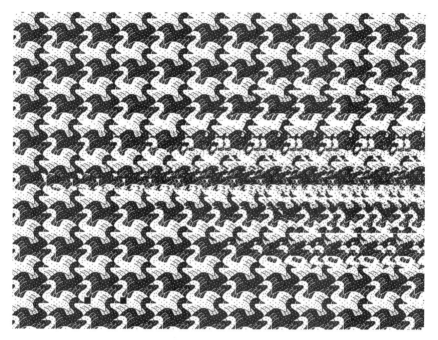

Figure 12: Magic Eye image

To demonstrate to Magic Eye readers how they could learn to see the 3D images, the creators provided a three-stage set of instructions. First, they presented a model – a visual representation – showing the mechanics and science behind the imaging. You will see in Figure 13 that the eye can focus on different planes so we can get two different focal points. Because of our binocular vision each eye will see a slightly different image. Our brain then merges them together, tricking us into thinking we see only one same image.

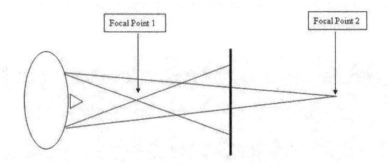

Figure 13: How Magic Eye imaging works

The second stage of the instructions involved explaining the *process* with a description of the various steps involved in being able to see the 3D images. They explained that when you initially view the picture, your eyes will focus on the page in the normal way and all you see are the repeated graphics. But if you focus with crossed eyes, (Focal point 1), the 3D picture will (hopefully) jump out at you. If you focus past the picture, (Focal point 2) the 3D image will retreat on the page. The third and final stage – and perhaps the most important – involves learning how to train your mind by developing the *habits* that enable you to instantly focus your eyes in the way described above and reveal the hidden 3D image.

So, to summarize the instructions for what's required to override our perceptive biases, the three steps are:

1. Visualize the *model*
2. Understand the *process*
3. Learn the *habits* that support the process

In Chapter 2, I discussed how our personal paradigms filter the world in such a way that what we perceive may not necessarily be the world as it is. That means we don't see things as they are, we see them as *we* are. So, to avoid frozen thinking and change the way we perceive the world, we need to change the way we think. It's not surprising we resort to frozen thinking. We solve problems the same way we always have, because we know those methods work. We drive or walk to work or school the same way we always do, because we know those ways get us to where we want to go. We spend our time doing more or less the same things and think in patterns that align with the ones we always have.

Model – process – habits. Sound familiar? So now let's compare this with what we have covered so far in this book and relate these learnings to how the three-step set of instructions may apply to cognitive filtering.

In Chapter 4, I introduced the Creative Monk Model which allows us to visualize what 20-20 Thinking looks like. We then examined the first half of the six-step C-R-E-A-T-E process that builds the foundations for creative thinking and ideation. Now comes the hard part – learning (and practicing) the habits to train our brain to think differently so we can engage in thought excursions.

As explained in Chapter 1, most people find individual or intra-personal change quite difficult. This involves changing the way we perceive things or changing the way in which we think. This is why many people can't see the *Magic Eye* images, and similarly, it's why many people may struggle to engage in thought excursions. Change from within is difficult – but it's not impossible. I know because I've done it, and all of the practicing creators have done it and continue to do it every day.

Training our mind to think and reason differently is really no different from training to achieve any goal. It requires perseverance, determination, and adopting the correct techniques. We also must be genuinely motivated to change as a half-hearted attempt isn't likely to sustain the kind of hard work required to make a real difference.

Daydream Believer

In the previous chapter, we saw that creativity is a habit that can be practiced, a muscle to be flexed. Now that you're familiar with strategies to help produce creative thought, it's time to address two important components that "power" that process. They are **atmosphere** and **thought excursions**; the "A" and "T" of the C-R-E-**A**-**T**-E process. Later in this chapter, we also cover the final stage of the process: **execution.**

Creativity shows itself in unpredictable ways, and you're going to find yourself following ideas along paths you never thought you'd tread. Consider the words commonly attributed to Charles H. Duell, Commissioner of the US Patent Office in 1899, when he is said to have claimed that "Everything that can be invented has been invented." If we look at the world today and its complex inventions, or at the ways art and music and literature have evolved since 1899, the advancements and changes are infinite. But if we see only what has come before us, it does still feel plausible to suggest that at some point we will reach all possible combinations of these existing elements. But now let's look at a classic example of how even the most seemingly obvious ideas are far from being apparent.

Bernard D. Sadow was Vice President of a Massachusetts luggage company. If anyone had ever lived and breathed baggage design and innovation it was Bernard – he was a truly dedicated and faithful employee. But it was when Bernard was returning from vacation in Aruba with his wife and kids and as they were going through customs in Puerto Rico while wrestling with two large, tightly packed 27-inch suitcases, and without a porter in sight, when he spotted a man moving a piece of machinery on a wheeled platform. Then he said to his wife, "That's what we need! We need wheels on luggage." Immediately upon return to work he set about designing a prototype. He attached four casters, like those used on trunks, to the bottom of a suitcase and added a flexible strap, and off to market he went, with a suitcase trailing behind him.

Sadow showed his new suitcase invention to every department store in New York City and everybody thought he was crazy. "Nobody's going to pull a piece of luggage with wheels on it. People just didn't think in those terms," Sadow recalled in an interview with CNN on the suitcase's 40th anniversary. Finally, Macy's Vice President was impressed with his idea and a product was born. He was so excited by his invention he *bought* the company he worked for. Sadow applied for and was granted a patent on wheeled suitcases. Macy's sold the first suitcases in October 1970 and the way people travelled changed forever.

Now think of the significance of this event. Wheeled suitcases are so convenient and so intuitively simple that they're an unremarkable essential for today's traveler. But to add a little perspective consider this, we managed to put a person on the moon earlier than it took to invent rolling luggage. Wheels have been around since pre-history and wheelbarrows for thousands of years. And yet for all the research and development that luggage businesses had put into improving their products, to win business and gain an edge over their competitors, no one had thought of the intuitively simple combination of wheels on a suitcase.

It took nearly 20 years for the next advance in rolling luggage. In 1987, the now ubiquitous rollaboard suitcase made its first appearance in airport terminals after a resourceful Northwest Airlines 747 pilot named Bob Plath came up with the bright idea to turn his suitcase upright, add on a couple of extra full-caster wheels, and insert a pull-up handle. Both these advances in the way we now travel relate to thinking differently and piecing together new combinations of things and ideas that already existed. As we saw in the previous chapter, 20-20 Thinking is about focusing on function rather than form when solving problems.

Now let's go back in time and consider an alternative scenario. Just suppose that Bernard D. Sadow and a bunch of his creative employees had locked themselves in a room and brainstormed the concept; What is the *function* of a travel suitcase? They would probably have come up with something along the lines of: "Its function is to get the contents of the suitcase from A to B in the most effective manner." In hindsight, the idea of attaching wheels to a suitcase shouldn't have been such a monumental breakthrough. The invention took more than 30 years of commercial air travel to happen just because people were stuck in the way they think, and as we have discovered throughout this book, resorted to frozen thinking.

What we gain from Bernard Sadow's story and his ah-ha moment at Puerto Rico Airport is that there is something very special about being in your "space-time" oasis when coming up with creative ideas. The two components of the C-R-E-A-T-E process of *atmosphere* and *thought excursions* are the prerequisites to creating your own space-time oasis. The two terms are related in that it requires the creation of the right atmosphere to promote thought excursions. It's only when we have created the right atmosphere that we can engage in thought excursions and this is what powers the Creative Triad. As we discovered in Chapter 3, thought excursions require us to extend our imagination. Much like creativity, imagination isn't a rare gift that only few possess. It is, however, greatly undervalued.

For many, imagination conjures up ideas of childishness, immaturity, or even delusion. As adults, we dismiss daydreaming as irrational and silly. We all have the ability to imagine brilliant, exciting things, but we choose to ignore this part of ourselves. Although daydreaming may seem mindless, a 2012 study suggested it could actually involve a highly engaged brain state. Daydreaming can lead to sudden connections and insights because it's related to our ability to recall information in the face of distractions. Neuroscientists have also found that daydreaming involves the same brain processes associated with imagination and creativity so it can aid in the process of creative incubation. And as most of us know from experience, our best, most creative ideas usually come seemingly out of the blue when our minds are elsewhere.

By engaging in thought excursions throughout the creative process, we open our minds up to new and different ways of thinking, combining pieces of information that haven't been combined before, and reach the space of change that is 20-20 Thinking. This chapter will show you that the path towards creativity isn't always clear. You never know how you're going to get to your next big idea, but by opening your mind, you can make sure you're ready when it arrives. It's only by leaving behind what is ordinary that we find the extraordinary.

Un-filtering our lives

Our minds unconsciously restrict our ability to come up with creative ideas or solutions because of the operation of the cognitive filters that the world and our environment has been shaped and developed in us over time. Each day, some neural responses are strengthened while others suppressed. The result is a brain well adapted to its environment but wired to interpret the world through the lens of what has happened in the past. This allows us to rapidly deal with familiar situations, but it can constrain us from solving unfamiliar or abstract encounters.

Recall from the McGurk Effect how our visual sensory processes overrode our auditory processes in that what we *saw* distorted the reality of the situation in hearing something we ought not to have heard. The McGurk Effect demonstrates the extent to which our cognitive biases filter our perceptions. The overwhelming dominance of our sense of sight is so powerful that our unconscious censors prohibit us from hearing the actual sound because it violates what our filtered senses perceive.

Our cognitive filtering devices focus our attention on the systems, images, and patterns that reflect our paradigms. The things we perceive are therefore consistent with the things we expect to perceive because we synthesize the information in a structured and organized manner based on past experiences. In the McGurk Effect, the image of the positioning of the speaker's lips is consistent with our inherent order of the way we process information, and so the sound we *think* we hear is consistent with the sound we *expect* to hear.

To progress along our path to a new way of thinking, the real difficulty we face now is learning how to cleanse ourselves of who we are. On the surface, this sounds like quite a daunting task. Because of who we are and the paradigms we keep, we hear these McGurk things we shouldn't hear, and we can't see the *Magic Eye* images we should see. Because frozen thinking constrains how we process information, the only way to move forward is to unshackle the impediments that keep our thoughts firmly rooted in our familiar environment. To quote Jimmy Cliff, "I can see clearly now the rain has gone, I can see all obstacles in my way."

If we can see these impediments, the path ahead requires that all obstacles be removed, and we come to the logical realization – or perhaps even revelation – that creating the ideal atmosphere for thought excursions is all about subtraction. In this age of information overload and unabated connectivity, those who lead a happier and more content life will be those who figure out what to leave out, so they can concentrate on what's important to them. One of the most wonderful human creations of all time supports this premise. When Pope Julius II asked Michelangelo about the secret of his genius in the creation of his statue of David, Michelangelo replied, "It's simple; I just took away everything that wasn't David."

Now let's start creating *our* atmosphere by removing those obstacles.

Atmosphere

We live our lives vicariously through a continuous sequence of revolving scenes. As Shakespeare once proclaimed: "All the world's a stage, And all the men and women merely players." Each act and each scene is played out in a different setting – a different atmosphere. The script remains essentially the same: work–home–sleep–repeat. It's only the scenery that changes – new job, different friends or, if you're lucky enough, another holiday destination. The stage rotates the scenery changes and our lives roll on. But what if we used these scene changes as a catalyst to create something entirely novel. Or better still, why not take on the role as director and create your own scene. Rather than continuing with our life-programmed script, what if we used our new scene as the stage to start something completely different – something entirely creative.

When I experienced my corona event in 2006, although I didn't appreciate it at the time, what I had fallen into was the perfect atmosphere for engaging in thought excursions. Now that I reflect on that time and my situation, I realize that the reason why that environment was so conducive to creativity was because all the impediments and obstacles opposing creativity had been removed from my life. The pressures and stress of my full-time job – gone! Internet and cell phone communications and distractions – non-existent or very limited at best. Challenges of raising three teenage children – what challenges? Virtually overnight my world had been transformed and my life had become simpler and far less complicated. I was not consciously trying to be creative, it just happened because I now had the time and space to let it happen. And so, it did.

What I was perfecting there on that small tropical island was a practice that I now call thought excursions. We examined thought excursions in Chapter 3 and explained them in terms of focusing on your concept, shaping an aspiration in your imagination, and integrating it into the reservoirs of information in both your conscious and unconscious mind, and then, in your atmosphere – your space-time oasis – allowing these ideas and creative elements to break into your consciousness. My space-time moments would happen when I was swimming laps in the pool or sipping on my Tusker Beer while watching the sunset over Port Vila lagoon or thinking of my loved ones far to the west, but mostly, it happened when I was asleep. The more I thought about *how* I was thinking, the more it allowed me to map out the blueprint for my 20-20 Thinking process.

I realized that creating the "right" atmosphere was a fundamental pre-requisite to the entire process of thinking differently. Great ideas don't happen in a vacuum. Just as humans need an atmosphere to breathe, so too do ideas. Take away the atmosphere and everything dies.

The reason why I recollected the first time I explored thought excursions in Vanuatu is because many people think – in fact, I was one of them – that a creative environment needs to be some far away exotic location, some idyllic seascape or perhaps a tropical isle like the one just described. This is not necessarily the case. What I experienced in Vanuatu that made it so conducive to making the "ideal" environment for creating was more about what I left behind rather than what I discovered there. What I now realize is that creativity comes from within so what's key to producing the ideal atmosphere for creating is to take away the things that are preventing it from surfacing. Vanuatu after all is an island – so if you didn't bring it with you, you're not going to find it there. But there are much easier ways of creating your ideal creative atmosphere than jetting off to a tropical paradise.

For some, traveling may provide inspiration, but it's by no means an essential element of the creative process. In fact, an effective creative atmosphere need not – and should not – be as complicated and convoluted as the one described above, and is likely far better if it's not. J.K. Rowling wrote most of *Harry Potter and the Philosopher's Stone* in an Edinburgh pub. Other authors gain creative inspiration while on the move, like spy novelist, John le Carré, who wrote many of his books while traveling on a train, and Gertrude Stein who preferred to write in her Model T. Ford. After being forced to resign from his job at the University of Mississippi, Nobel Prize winner, William Faulkner, worked a night shift at a power plant to make ends meet, and it was at this plant that he wrote his epic novel, *As I Lay Dying*. Clearly, everyone's creative atmosphere is very much a case of horses for courses. Irrespective or where or when it is, your creative atmosphere should be constructed so that it's as easily replicable as possible – so that you can access it as and when you need it. Like most other sought-after things in life, creating a creative atmosphere is all about planning.

The project management adage of "plan your work and work your plan" is equally applicable to the task of devising your own creative atmosphere. Without too much effort, you can start arranging the environmental and psychological variables to form an atmosphere conducive to thought excursions that will enhance the promotion and development of creative ideas. Once you've determined what your space-time oasis looks like, you can habitually recreate it at your leisure. Therefore, the starting point is all about the planning. It's about arranging the scenery on your personal stage to create an environment conducive to getting those creative juices flowing. And the most efficient way to set about the task of creating your environment is to make the most of where you now are and your current circumstances.

But first let's revisit our 20-20 Thinking model.

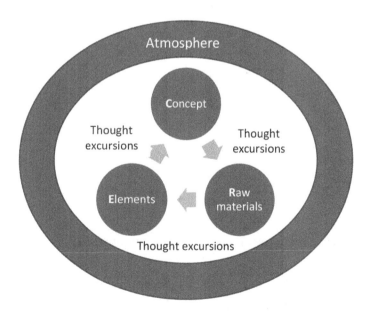

Figure 14: The C-R-E-A-T-E Process

Recall Einstein's revelation: "the formulation of a problem is far more essential than its solution." What's most important in the 20-20 Thinking process is to create a personalized atmosphere that's conducive to promoting creativity. In Figure 14 the concept is your problem, your goal or the wrong you want to right. From Chapter 3, we saw that in the C-R-E-A-T-E process, it's your thought excursions that carry the raw materials continuously around the Creative Triad of concept – raw materials – elements. And all of this happens most effectively when encompassed within the right kind of atmosphere. Having created the right atmosphere allows more bits of information to circulate in your mind – some within your conscious and some from your subconscious.

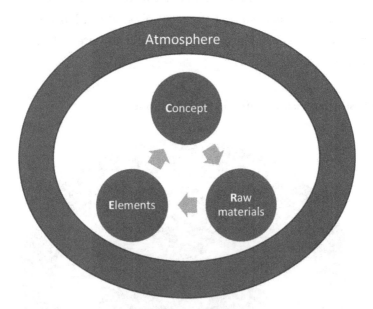

Figure 15: The Creative Triad: C-R-E

More dots mean there are more chances of random associations and more chance of joining those dots, and if that happens, you get your elements. The Creative Triad process continually develops and refines your concept until it's ready to be unleashed upon the world. And that's the time for execution – the transitioning your concept to reality.

It's important to note that there are no set of components that make up a model for a creative environment and there's no definitive creative atmosphere template to follow and simply generically apply for yourself. What works for some may not work for others. But one thing is certain is that the atmosphere you create needs to work for *you*.

Because of the criticality of constructing your own creative atmosphere I have provided the following four steps to assist you in creating an atmosphere that promotes and stimulates creative thinking.

Step 1: Location, location, location

> There are no set rules in the where or what of your location, however, finding the right location is more about being mindful of what the wrong location looks like. Your creative environment may be a table at your favorite café, that quiet little nook at home, or perhaps even your local library, but it needs to be the same place each time so that your senses are not distracted by new perceptions. The Creative Triad part of the 20-20 Thinking process is the most energy sapping as it requires you to concentrate intensely on trying to find relationship between all the bits of information as they relate to your concept, so you'll also need it to be comfortable and set aside specific time so you're not interrupted.
>
> Irrespective of where it is, claim it as your creative space. It's important that once you've decided on your location, make sure you only occupy this place when you want to create. When in this special place, don't even think of anything to do with work or any issues that are of concern to you. Think only of your concept.

Step 2: Mentally and physically disconnect from work

At work, we're not playful and our minds are usually in closed mode. And more often than not, we're far from being in a relaxed state of body or mind. So, much like finding the right physical location is important, so too does distancing yourself from the closed mindset of work. By separating work from play, you're priming your mind to be in a more playful state, and you'll feel more relaxed and content.

In some instances, this may just look like leaving the office or workplace and going to your chosen location. Yet, as the pandemic has shifted many traditional workplaces to accommodate working from home, the ability to disconnect from work has become far more challenging. If your location is at home, take away everything you associate with work. If possible, separate your "work" area from your "play" area. If your home doesn't allow for a physical separation, remove, or at least put out of sight, all those work things that will inevitably distract you.

Step 3: Remove distractions

Today's world is full of constant distractions and stimulation, and technology plays a massive role in this. As your brain hops from one interruption and notification to the next, constantly trying to keep up, creative ideas have no space to unfurl. So, to set up your creative atmosphere, you'll need to remove or turn off all disruptive technologies.

Zadie Smith, English novelist and Professor of Creative Writing at New York University has two tips for writing: "Protect the time and space in which you write," and "work on a computer that is disconnected from the internet." Turn off the television and put your cell phone on silent or put it out of sight. Audio-visual mediums appeal to our sense of sight and hearing and both senses are extremely effective in gaining our attention. You may also like to take off your watch as even glancing to check the time is sufficient to distract your thought processes. If your mind is occupied with distractions, that's enough to derail your 20-20 Thinking process.

Step 4: Set the right frame of mind

> When we're in a relaxed state, feeling content, and in a good mood, our mind is open to taking in what's around us. The long-standing view in psychology is that positive emotions are conducive to creativity because they broaden the mind, whereas negative emotions stifle creativity because they narrow one's focus. In a 2007 Rice University study, scientists looked explicitly at how positive and negative moods impact on creativity. The study found that "participants in positive moods demonstrate divergent thinking, fluid ideation, flexible categorization, make unusual associations, and perform well on insight problems, unusual word associations, and heuristic problem-solving tasks."

The pressing times of COVID-19's travel restrictions and self-isolation, or perhaps even losing or being furloughed from your job, is far from an ideal creative atmosphere. Feeling relaxed, content, and positive while living in the midst of a pandemic is not going to be likely. So, even if you don't feel like swinging from the chandeliers, stick to steps one to three and persevere in any case. The important thing is to get something down. At the end of the day, you can't edit a blank sheet of paper.

The Importance of Sensory Association

I'm sure there's a particular song that, when you hear it, it takes you back to a particular time and place. That song has a direct and inextricable link to an experience from your past. Hearing the song = reliving the moment. What's happening here is that subconsciously our senses associate with a particular happening or environment. For instance, when Pavlov's dogs heard the bell ringing, they would associate it with being fed and then reacted physiological to that stimulus. It's the same with your special location. When you return to your location and you perceive the unique combinations of sensory cues, you'll be returned to your creative mood.

It's not just our sense of sound and sight that are aroused when we're at our particular location either. A few years ago, I took my wife and children to stay in a stunning 16th century royal hunting lodge in Surrey that I'd visited when I was growing up in England some 45 years earlier. Yet, as soon as I walked through the large oak door into the main entrance room, I was immediately hit by a smell that took me back to that time in my childhood. It was the smell of a particular wood polish that was used to protect the 400-year-old furniture and staircase. When I made inquiry with the proprietors, they informed me that they had been using the same brand of polish for the past century. And with that sensory cue came flooding back other memories relating to that particular time and place. That single sensory association unlocked from my subconscious all those things that were associated with that time that would otherwise have remained dormant.

Our senses are amazingly selective. Research published in *Science* in 2012 found that humans can detect more than a trillion different smells. By comparison, our eyes can only distinguish a puny 2.3 to 7.5 million colors. Most of the scents we encounter are actually mixtures of tens to hundreds of different odorous molecules. The scent of a rose, for instance, is composed of over 275 distinct compounds. So, if our senses of sound, sight and smells can be so discerning and take us back to a particular time and place and draw upon our subconscious reservoir of information, why don't we use this innate feature of the human brain to instantly return us to our creative environment.

Reviving these memories also draws on the associated feelings and emotions that you relate to that scene. What emotions stir when you hear "My Heart Will Go on" and you think of *that* scene in *Titanic*. And what about that iconic scene in *Ghost* with Demi Moore and Patrick Swayze and their nocturnal pot-throwing of the phallic clay with the Righteous Brothers' cover of "Unchained Melody" playing. It will certainly bring back a different feeling and emotion when you hear Julie Andrews singing "The Hills are Alive" on a scenic alpine meadow in *The Sound of Music* or the Bee Gees singing "Stayin' Alive" in *Saturday Night Fever*. These examples demonstrate that by combining two or more sensory associations, the reinforcement of that scene or experience is even greater. Our senses play an enormous part in consciousness. Senses provide important data to the storage vaults of both our conscious and unconscious mind. What is a memory without the sight, sound, smell, taste, and feel of the memory?

Summarizing what you should do

The selection of the location of your creative oasis matters less than the atmosphere surrounding that environment – so hold off on booking your flight to the Maldives. Your mind will store and categorize all those sensory cues to ensure they will associate that place with your creative space-time oasis. If all you do at your creative oasis is think and do creative things, then your mind will associate that environment and atmosphere with creativity and *only* creativity. This is why it's so important not to pollute your creative atmosphere with impediments or obstacles that may stifle your 20-20 Thinking process.

One last important thing to remember – it's also important not to go to your special location if you are not wanting to create. Sensory associations are strengthened more if they're positively reinforced. You want to preserve and protect your special oasis for the sole purpose of creating a haven for your 20-20 Thinking time. But remember, it takes time to develop creative associations, but it *will* happen – I can guarantee you that.

Preparing for Thought Excursions

Earlier in this chapter we discussed the importance of finding the right location for creating the ideal atmosphere for you to come up with creative ideas. The location you identified as your creative oasis is where you'll do the hard yards of consciously focusing on your concept or problem and trying to find ideas from remote associations of all the raw materials you gathered.

Now you're at the stage of looking for a second and different location where you can conduct your thought excursions. This is where you go *after* you've completely exhausted your efforts in trying to find relationships and association between your raw materials. This new location is where you go for resting and relaxing. Rest to energize your body and relaxation to prime your mind.

The bliss of solitude

Being alone means having the time and mental space to reflect on yourself, your experiences, and your ideas, all of which are necessary for the 20-20 Thinking process. Call it what you like – "incubation time" or "constructive internal reflection" – it's the time where you allow your mind to wander after you've taken new information in. Now you must allow your mind to rest to assimilate the information, but this is the time when you come up with new and better ideas. That's why it's important to make time for solitude, to give yourself space to reflect, make new connections, and find new meaning.

Unfortunately, solitude is widely undervalued, leading many people to shy away from alone time. Many western cultures tend to view time alone as time wasted or as an indication of antisocial behavior or a melancholy personality. But the ability to enjoy and make productive use of our own company is the secret to creativity that helps us tap into our thoughts and inner worlds. So, don't avoid it – embrace it! John Cleese provides an insightful account of the importance of restringing your mind as part of the creative process:

> ▌▌ *"This is the extraordinary thing about creativity, if you just keep your mind resting against the concept in a friendly but persistent way, sooner or later you will get a reward from your unconscious, probably in the shower later. Or at breakfast the next morning, but suddenly you are rewarded, out of the blue a new thought mysteriously appears."*

Setting aside the time for resting the mind is one thing but where do you go and what do you do during your time of solitude? For many, the answer is exercise. It therefore comes as no surprise that many creative and successful people build exercise into their daily routines. Virgin founder, Richard Branson, runs every morning, composers Beethoven and Tchaikovsky both walked daily, as does prolific author, Stephen King.

There's plenty of evidence pointing to the benefits of exercise for fueling the creative process. A Stanford University study found that 90 per cent of people were more creative after they exercised. In the 2014 study, 176 college students completed some creative thinking tasks. The research found that when people were walking, either on treadmills or outdoors, they were 60 per cent more creative than when idlily sitting around. So, exercising is good – wherever or however you may do it.

If exercising isn't your thing, there are a great many other options available. British Booker Prize-winning author, Hilary Mantel suggests:

> *"If you get stuck, get away from your desk. Take a walk, take a bath, go to sleep, make a pie, draw, listen to music, meditate, exercise; whatever you do, don't just stick there scowling at the problem. But don't make telephone calls or go to a party; if you do, other people's words will pour in where your lost words should be. Open a gap for them, create a space. Be patient."*

Where to conduct thought excursions

Ever since my corona event in 2006, I've actively partaken in metacognition – thinking about what I am thinking. I've come to the realization that there are a few special places that do it for me in terms of conducting these thought excursions. They may sound a bit strange but if you follow all the above steps in selecting your location then you may find some of your locations are equally weird.

One place I go for thought excursions is traveling on commercial airliners, which, before COVID-19, was quite often. I always plan for a window seat – doesn't matter what class, they all work perfectly fine. I put on my noise cancelling headphones – I don't need music playing, but if there is, it will be something familiar like, say, Pink Floyd's *Dark Side of the Moon* – then my favorite eye mask, and by the time the last door closes I'm off, both physically and creatively.

A few years back when I was on the inaugural direct 17-hour flight from Australia to England, I applied this technique and got an amazing amount of work done. Not just words, but more importantly, concepts and ideas.

Another special place for me is mowing the lawn on weekends. I'm not sure if it's the smell of the freshly cut grass or the sun on my back or the mechanical drone of the lawn mower; but whatever it is, it works. So much so that when I'm out mowing, I now carry a notebook and pen in my pocket and am constantly interrupted to jot down thoughts and ideas as they come to me.

Although my two creative environments are in stark contrast to each other, they have some common characteristics. With both I have deliberately and consciously put my concept or problem out of my mind before I start. I have no externally connected devices – no internet, no cell phone connectivity. I've gone to a place that I find pleasurable and relaxing. And with both, I know I'll have no external distractions or interruptions for a particular period of time – the length of the flight or however it takes to mow my lawn.

For some, your special place may be to take a long hike, during which your mind has nothing to worry about except putting one foot in front of the other. Perhaps it's going for a long drive where your primary focus is on the road. Whatever it is that works for you requires refocusing your attention on some activity other than your concept or problem.

Rest and relaxation

This step is probably the easiest one in the whole book. Drop the subject you're working on, stop gathering raw materials, and put your concept out of your mind. You, along with your conscious brain, have been working hard and it's time for the subconscious to do its thing. This means you need to schedule a time and place to turn off. It doesn't need to be immediately after you've stopped working on developing your ideas, but it needs to be at a time and location that works for you. The notion of thought excursions requires that you consciously set aside the problem or concept and redirect your attention to something enjoyable and relaxing. You become more aware of the true value of your time, not just as a currency to exchange for money, but something valuable to you personally, something to be invested in any way you deem the most meaningful. And investing it in a variety of passions can be the key to making your creativity soar.

Rest is commonly thought of as the opposite of work. We either rest or we're productive. Over the past decade, neuroscientists have discovered that solitary, inwardly focused reflection engages a different brain network than outwardly focused attention. When our mental focus is directed towards the outside world (top-down processing), as is the case when we're focusing on specific problems or performing mental calculations, the brain's high-level executive attention network is activated, and our imagination network is suppressed.

The associative processes of creative thinking don't thrive when our conscious mind is in a focused state and operating in closed mode. A relaxed and open mind explores novel ideas; an occupied mind searches for the most familiar ideas, which are usually the least interesting, least creative, and invariably of the least utility. For a long time, scientists assumed that the brain mostly powers down when we rest, like a computer or television going into the appropriately named "sleep" mode. However, neuroscientists have more recently observed something quite different. They've discovered that a mind at rest is anything but vacant. Rather than an overall decrease in activity, the activity just shifts to different parts of the brain. The parts of the brain that activate during rest are referred to as the Default Mode Network or DMN.

Further research conducted at the University of Southern California by neuroscientist Mary Immordino-Yang found that DMN activity is highly correlated with intelligence, empathy, emotional judgment, and even overall mental health. As the DMN kicks in, our intuition takes center stage and our creativity and problem-solving skills become more non-linear, making more distant associations. If you've ever had a powerful daydream or epiphany while on a walk or in the shower, you can thank your DMN for that. In a moment that feels restful to you, your DMN is quietly seeking out big-picture strategies for the problems you're trying to solve or the creative breakthrough you might be seeking.

This goes a long way in explaining why our best ideas tend to arise when our attention is not engaged on the outside world and we're in a mood of solitary reflection. This bottom-up mode of processing involves individual neurons firing in a complex manner without being dictated by input from the brain's executive structures. Unfortunately, as our default networks are marginalized more and more by the sheer pace of contemporary society, we have less unfocused time for our internal processes to progress. As a result, we have less opportunity to piece together those random associations that lead to new ideas and realizations.

Albert Einstein was known to escape the distractions of the everyday world by heading out on the open water sailing or playing the violin. It was in these moments, whilst alone, where many of his greatest discoveries came to him. For Einstein, playing the violin and sailing, the two things he most loved to do, allowed him to disappear. As Einstein explained, it was during these pleasurable pursuits that his unconscious mind would go on thinking about the challenge and surprise even himself with a breakthrough insight or innovation at the time when he least expected it.

According to French mathematician and philosopher, Henri Poincaré, to lubricate the machinery of unconscious ideation, we must "first prime the mind with directed conscious work, then relieve it of its standard inhibitions." In the previous chapter, we looked at the "directed conscious work" in the form of the Creative Triad. It was the continuous cycle of developing your concept, gathering raw materials, and forming the elements. It's now within this new and different atmosphere that we have purposely created to embark upon thought excursions that allow our subconscious to perform the difficult task of identifying relationships and establishing bonds (that is, forming *elements*) between the vast volume of information we've gathered.

Harvesting the Subconscious

I didn't realize it at the time, but what I was perfecting just after I'd experienced my corona event was a practice I call "disciplined" or "intentional" dreaming. It's where I go to conduct my thought excursions. But unlike my "daytime" thought excursion locations, in which I completely put out of my mind my concept or problem I'm working on, in bed, I intensely focus upon my concept, shaping an aspiration in my imagination before I go to sleep and integrating it into the reservoirs of my unconscious before I dream. This is where and how some of my most creative ideas have been born and that has shaped the direction of my life. As Victor Hugo so put it, "There is nothing like a dream to create the future."

What we do every day when we're consciously perceiving the world is drawing upon our memory. Sometimes, with the routine things we do, we develop habits that effectively bypass our memory and consciousness. But even during these mundane activities, we draw enormously on the vast reservoir of information that's stored in our subconscious mind. It contains our most recent memories, our feelings, and the habits we rely on. Our conscious mind may tell us we have to drive to that 11 o'clock appointment, but the habits within our subconscious mind start the car, select drive mode, and stop and start us till we get to our appointment. We've all had that experience where we step out of the car and remember very little about the drive. That's our subconscious at work. The conscious draws on the subconscious all day long — calling up names to faces, future plans, and developing strategies for problem-solving.

With every decision we make, at any time of the day, the subconscious mind works underneath our conscious mind to add texture to our lives without us even realizing. It's the enormous cloud server to our conscious mind's smartphone. In essence, what we're attempting to do through disciplined dreaming is to integrate all levels of consciousness while we sleep. We want to master our consciousness. Through disciplined dreaming, we are using the conscious mind to influence our other layer of consciousness: our subconscious. So now let's take a closer look at what's going on when we are sleeping.

All of the information that runs through the subconscious mind requires a fair amount of time to itself to sort out what's important and what's not. This sorting and categorizing of thoughts and memories are what we experience as dreams. For thousands of years, we've looked to dreams as important visions, gifts from the gods. But what we need to realize is that the information being delivered in them to us is our own subconscious mind. The way dreams seem to move through different scenes, how you can be sitting in your bedroom one minute and running through a field of daffodils the next without noticing a transition, is a product of the subconscious mind moving through different memories, spontaneously making remotely associated connections. It's in this dream space that our brain can sometimes surprise us, bringing back problems that have been plaguing us and looking at them from a new angle.

One of Paul McCartney's most treasured creations for The Beatles is the song, *Yesterday*, yet the piece was a product of his subconscious. In 1964, McCartney woke up with a melody in his head. Finding the chords that could bring it to life, he took this dream and worked with it until it became one of the most played songs of all time.

With its ability to push forward new perspectives and its remarkable processing power, the subconscious seems like the ideal tool for generating creative thought, but it's not quite as simple as waiting for the best ideas to find you while you sleep. Paul McCartney couldn't have gone to bed thinking, "well, time to write my next big hit!" Nor could he afford to sit around waiting for an album's worth of dream melodies to appear out of nowhere. Counting on the subconscious mind to generate ideas can be unpredictable at best, but there are habits you can practice to create the ideal atmosphere for your subconscious to engage with. In achieving this atmosphere, you can prime your mind and make sure it's as receptive as possible to the next creative thought, no matter how weird.

Priming the mind

Henri Poincaré was an early advocate for the creative powers of the subconscious mind. His approach to work was likened to a bee flying from one flower to the next. Poincaré admitted that he never spent a long time on any particular problem as he believed that the subconscious mind would continue working on the problem while he consciously worked on another problem, got a good night's sleep, or savored a glass of Beaujolais.

To facilitate these habits, Poincaré worked in two short bursts of two hours every day, from 10am to 12pm and from 5pm to 7pm. While this might sound like a particularly light workload, Poincaré believed that virtually all of his time was spent working, just not in a traditional sense. He believed in using this time to prime his mind, establishing his mathematical conundrum he was working on within it, and he would then set about creating the atmosphere to enable his subconscious to unfurl the solution. Key to ensuring his subconscious did this, he believed, was the removal of the inhibitions of the conscious mind. Poincaré explains:

> "One evening, contrary to my custom, I drank black coffee and could not sleep. Ideas rose in crowds; I felt them collide until pairs interlocked, so to speak, making a stable combination. It seems, in such cases, that one is present at his own unconscious work, made partially perceptible to the over-excited consciousness, yet without having changed its nature."

This account appears to be very similar to our C-R-E-A-T-E process and the Creative Triad when two remote bits of information combine to form an element. All happening within the subconscious but with guidance and direction from our consciousness.

Poincaré was not the only advocate for the creative potential of disciplined dreaming. At the turn of the last century, most scientists believed that nerve impulses were transmitted electrically, like telegraph signals. Otto Loewi, a German-born physiologist, had the idea that they might be transmitted chemically. He was at a loss how to prove it, though, and let the idea slip to the back of his mind. But in 1920, he had a dream:

> "The night before Easter Sunday of that year I awoke, turned on the light, and jotted down a few notes on a tiny slip of paper. Then I fell asleep again. It occurred to me at 6 o'clock in the morning that during the night I had written down something most important, but I was unable to decipher the scrawl. The next night, at 3 o'clock, the idea returned. It was the design of an experiment to determine whether or not the hypothesis of chemical transmission that I had uttered 17 years ago was correct. I got up immediately, went to the laboratory, and performed a single experiment on a frog's heart according to the nocturnal design."

It took Loewi another decade to carry out a decisive series of tests to satisfy his critics, but ultimately his initial dream-induced experiment led to proof that nerve impulses are indeed chemically transmitted. As a child, Otto Loewi never even imagined he'd become a scientist. And yet as a scientist he went on to become a world-leading expert in physiology, and for his efforts was awarded the Nobel Prize in Medicine. And all because of a wild dream.

Dreamtime is such an important part of the 20-20 Thinking process. In many respects preparing for your nocturnal thought excursions is similar to how we prepared our atmosphere as discussed earlier in this chapter. There are four steps involved:

1. Preparing your sleep atmosphere
2. Getting into the right frame of mind
3. Making the most of waking up
4. Repeating the process

Step 1. Preparing your sleep atmosphere

> *Remember, creativity is all about subtraction. So, take away the distractors in your room. Don't have those blue light devices (laptop, tablet, phone) on for at least a half-hour before you go to sleep. Blue light keeps you up and, depending on the content you have been dealing with (for example, the news), it may increase your anxiety. Kill the TV, leave your cell phone and laptop in another room, and take your smart watch off. Make sure your sleeping space is as quiet as possible. And don't forget to have that notebook and pencil on your bedside table.*

Step 2. Getting into the right frame of mind

Preparing your mind presupposes that your body is already prepared. Deep breathing or a hot bath or shower before you go to bed may help get your body and mind in a relaxed state ready for sleep. However you get there, keep your anxieties and worries out of the bedroom. Don't go to bed with a tight body and mind.

Once in bed, review your concept or aspiration in your mind. Perceive it in your imagination. What does the realization of your concept look like? Think of the monks forever climbing and descending those stairs. Bring as much form and sensory awareness you can to the process. Is there a fragrance to it? Is there an associated sound or sight? Once you've visualized your concept and have it firmly planted in your upper consciousness, dive now straight down into the depths of your subconsciousness.

Good night and pleasant dreams.

Step 3. Making the most of waking up

> I don't know about you, but I've never felt especially ready to work when I'm still waking up. This period of coming out of sleep is called the hypnopompic state. We often end up with strong visual images lingering from our dreams when we wake out of REM (Rapid Eye Movement) sleep when most of our dreaming happens. For this reason, lots of artists have coveted this just-waking-up period to improve their creative thinking. Surrealist artist Salvador Dalí, was renowned for making the most of waking time to help him generate creative ideas. He would often nap in a chair, holding a spoon in his hand and under the spoon, on the floor, was a tin plate. When he drifted off to sleep, he'd drop the spoon, with the clattering noise it made on the plate waking him and allowing him to latch onto those vivid images that occur in his dreams.
>
> Poincaré described lying in bed in a half-dream state as the ideal condition for coming up with new ideas. The philosopher and mathematician René Descartes famously loved to lounge in bed in the morning and think. It was on one such morning – so the story goes – while dreamily watching the path of a fly darting around on the ceiling, that Descartes came up with the x-y plane of Cartesian coordinates.
>
> Don't worry if you can't recall your dreams. You might, but you might not. There's always tomorrow night.

Step 4. Repeating the process

▌▌ Repeat the process every night. If Otto Loewi had not repeated the process the following night after his forgotten dream, he may never have become a Nobel Prize laureate. Repeat the process and continue to repeat it. That may be a few days, weeks, years or perhaps even a single lifetime. For the past decade, I've thought about the concept of this book. Regardless of the duration, the purpose of this exercise is about heightening your sense of intuition in your waking life. Somehow you will "know" when it has been enough. Maybe there's another concept that takes priority. Your brain, with its some 2.5 petabytes capacity, is quite capable of handling more than one concept at a time. But above all, it's important to retain a playful attitude rather than a passionate one. It's not "I must have this, or my life is over," it's more like, "let's have fun with this!"

Some Concluding Thoughts on your Space-Time Oasis

For us to engage in effective 20-20 Thinking, I cannot overstate enough just how critical it is to create the right atmosphere and find your special space-time oasis for conducting thought excursions. We must do as Poincaré suggests and unburden the conscious mind and stem the overwhelming tide of information from reaching the brain. Ultimately, it's up to you to figure out what practices are most effective for you to rid your mind of distractions and engage the subconscious.

When it comes to figuring out how to find your space-time oasis, start by interrogating your existing routine. Ask yourself: are there times of the day or days of the week when you feel you think more clearly than others? Are there activities that tend to calm you or help bring about your best ideas? Conversely, are there activities that tend to leave you flustered or mentally overloaded? Perhaps, like the Paul McCartney and Henri Poincaré, you find ideas coming to you in the peaceful state of sleep. Or maybe you're like Agatha Christie, who is said to have had all her best ideas in the bath while eating apples and drinking tea. Whatever it is, ensure that when creating the atmosphere and location for your thought excursions, you focus on the world around you as well as within your head. Avoiding external distractions seems the most obvious, but it's also important to recognize when the distractions are the result of your own unfocused mind.

In the past two decades, as the internet, and social media in particular, have grown to overtake nearly all aspects of our lives, we've been bombarded with information. To keep up, we've developed the ability to skim, to coast along the top of these constant waves of information, getting a general sense of most of it without stopping to focus on any one thing. Think about it: when you're scrolling through a site like Facebook and see a news article, how often do you stop to open and read it? How often do you read the headline and move on, making conclusions from that information alone? If you do click on an article, do you read and digest every word, or do you skim the first sentences of the paragraphs, before skipping to the end for some kind of summary? Although the increased spread of fake news has raised the moral panic of not doing your own research before drawing conclusions, this is simply the only way we can stay on top of this crazy world without becoming overloaded. We've had to learn to juggle multiple thoughts at once, to make decisions based on a multitude of stimuli in the blink of an eye.

In this fast-paced digital world, our brain takes in information at a rate that the conscious mind struggles to keep up with. Luckily for us, behind this lies the powerful, albeit mysterious, subconscious mind. But if the part of the mind that takes in information at the speed of a supercomputer were given more of a break, we would begin to see more interesting results. In finding a more nurturing atmosphere for the subconscious, we can enter a state conducive to 20-20 Thinking, and in particular, our thought excursions. Disconnecting from distraction and the pressure of trying to be creative, we open the subconscious mind to working with the conscious mind and bringing out creative solutions to problems once considered out of reach.

The subconscious mind is unpredictable, and quite often strange, so you'll need to be ready to accept that. When your subconscious throws out a vision of you chasing a beam of light, for example, follow that thought along until you've reached the question that challenges established notions of relativity. Thought excursions are, for this reason, a mindset first and a process second. To delve into the imaginary and find the answers you seek, you need to value those thoughts you've been told your whole life to dismiss as childish whimsy. Embrace them, cherish them, and nurture them.

Execution

Finally, we've come to the end of our C-R-E-A-T-E process in having arrived at the second E: **execution**. In our C-R-E-A-T-E process, the term refers to the act of doing or performing something in a planned way. Execution is the final act of transforming out concept into reality. In his micro-masterpiece, Young refers to this last stage of the creative thought process as "the cold, grey dawn of the morning after." This is when your newborn idea has to face the world of reality.

Although the realization or otherwise of your concept becoming reality depends on this stage of the process, the guidance I can provide on how to do this is quite limited. The reason for this is because the variety and diversity of the subject matter of you concept is limited only by your imagination. Therefore, the execution strategies are, likewise, infinite. It would be fitting to reference here Albert Einstein when he said: "Two things are infinite: the universe and human stupidity; and I'm not sure about the universe."

As we saw in Chapter 4, we need to construct our concept logically and consciously, but its solutions are quite often resolved intuitively in the subconscious mind. It's only now, at the final stage of the creative thought process, that we return to the harsh veracity of the real world.

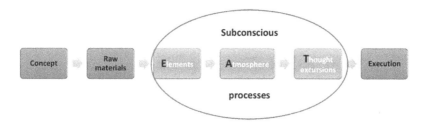

Figure 16: Thinking consciously and subconsciously

As shown in Figure 16, it's back to the rational and the linear for the final component of the C-R-E-A-T-E process. Einstein maintained that "the application of logic and the use of words are useful when it comes to developing concepts and their execution but ineffective when attempting to explain the concepts and realizing creative breakthroughs." You can look at execution as either the beginning or the end. A great (creative) idea can fail because it hasn't been properly executed. Consider international bestselling author John Gresham's first novel, *A Time to Kill*, which was rejected by dozens of publishing houses in New York before eventually being taken up by a very small and unknown publisher. It sold less than 500 copies and then mostly to friends and relatives. After the release of his highly acclaimed second novel, *The Firm*, his original novel, without a *single* changed word, sold in excess of 3 million copies. The book was unchanged – the concept remained as it was – but because of a different set of circumstances its second execution was entirely different.

Something that would otherwise have been a failure became an amazing success story and established the literary career of one of the world's most prolific and successful authors.

From a personal perspective I've experienced the difference between an effective and non-effective execution of a concept. While writing this book, I came up with the concept of starting a domestic airline at a time when the airline industry was in freefall with COVID-19 restrictions closing international borders and curbing domestic travel. Experts predicted that half of the world's airlines would not survive.

Thirty years ago, I had the idea of launching a domestic airline, under what was then far more favorable conditions. But I was wrong. In fact, apart from the concept, everything I did in terms of executing the concept was wrong. I was laboring under the naïve notion that if an idea was good enough – and I mean *really* good enough – then that would be sufficient to guarantee its success. Not true to the nth degree. I struggle to imagine how many other J K Rowling's or Arctic Monkeys' there are out there but failed on the last hurdle in getting the execution right. But those who persevered have all made it – and so can you!

In terms of execution of a concept, what may seem logical using traditional thinking techniques may be viewed as bizarre under 20-20 Thinking, and vice versa. But this time, in applying 20-20 Thinking to my concept, I realized that there was no better time to launch a new domestic airline than during a pandemic. The radically changed global environment, brought about by the coronavirus pandemic, had presented unprecedented opportunities. Under these changed conditions, the lease price of modern jet aircraft reduced by up to one quarter of what it was pre-COVID, highly trained and experienced pilots and other aviation professionals were now readily available for employment having been stood-down from other failing or collapsed airlines, and allocated times to access busy airports became available with airport operators crying out for client airlines. All these factors are critical in driving down the cost of operating commercial airline services and, in a post-COVID world, airfare pricing will undoubtedly be the number-one determinant of which airline people will fly domestically. Airlines established and structured upon these changed operating conditions will have an amazingly competitive advantage over their rivals.

It's all a matter of the timing, manner, and style of the execution of your concept that determines whether it will succeed or fail. It is possible to turn a global catastrophe into a prime opportunity to follow your dreams, turning 2020's lemons into next year's lemonade–provided you get the execution right.

In a dramatically restructured economy and society, old assumptions and traditional marketing strategies won't get us back on our feet, but thinking creatively will. Having new and creative ideas is awesome but are meaningless if they aren't effectively executed. The final step of the C-R-E-A-T-E process is all about turning our creative concept into reality but to do this our *mode of execution* must be based on creative ideas. So, our *new* concept becomes: How do I execute my concept? This now becomes our *new* concept – and so the C-R-E-A-T-E process begins afresh.

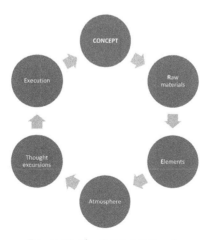

Figure 17: The C-R-E-A-T-E cycle

What better way of ensuring that our execution will be effective than guaranteeing it will be creative.

And so, we start the process all over again . . .

Learnings from Chapter 5:

Great ideas need space and time and a lot of deep thinking. No matter how counterintuitive that may feel, sometimes it's best to sit back, relax and let an idea breathe. We take in enough information every day to drown out all of our own thoughts. Prioritize disconnecting from that avalanche of information and disruptive technologies. Don't be afraid to follow the bizarre thoughts and bring back the child in you – sometimes those are the most interesting. But after all the hard work and effort, make sure you get the execution right; after all, that determines whether or not your concept will be realized.

Now go to **Chapter 6 – Habits** and relate the above learnings to the following habits:
- Habit #9 Do you feel deeply?
- Habit #10 Do you sometimes think and behave like a child?

6

HABITS TO SUPPORT 20-20 THINKING

"Excellence is a habit."

Aristotle

What is the difference between a trait and a habit? In the great nature versus nurture debate, a trait corresponds to your nature, while a habit can be nurtured. So, can a habit become a trait? Consider how something you do on a regular basis can become a part of your identity. If you paint every morning or jog every afternoon, you become "the painter" or "the jogger" and if you tell enough half-truths you may even become "the politician." Creativity is a combination of both nature and nurture, a habit nurtured to become a trait.

From infancy, we're born curious about the world around us, but for some, that natural curiosity is worn away and conditioned out through rigid schooling systems or other institutions that don't take kindly to new ways of thinking. As adults, we need to learn or even re-learn how to harness our natural curiosity to produce something new. As Austrian Professor Emeritus, Helga Nowotny wrote in her book, *Insatiable Curiosity: Innovation in a Fragile Future*, curiosity pushes us into new territory.

> "Curiosity, insatiable as it is, drives us forward. It seeks new paths and willingly accepts that some are wrong turns. It seeks risk, thereby repeatedly staking what it has already found and achieved. Again and again, it subverts limits that have been reached to fence them in or guide them in certain directions. It poses questions that are not permitted, and unwise as it is, it presses for action even where it should draw back."

"Curiosity, insatiable as it is, drives us forward. It seeks new paths and willingly accepts that some are wrong turns. It seeks risk, thereby repeatedly staking what it has already found and achieved. Again and again, it subverts limits that have been reached to fence them in or guide them in certain directions. It poses questions that are not permitted, and unwise as it is, it presses for action even where it should draw back."

With an open heart and curious mind, we all can find and create the changes we wish to see in ourselves. To help cultivate this, through extensive research I've compiled the following 10 habits that will nurture creativity, re-awaken your curiosity in the world and your life, and help drive your motivation and resolve to create your own new normal.

How to use this chapter

Within each of the 10 sub-headings in this chapter, I will expand further on the 10 habits introduced throughout this book. Each section in this chapter will provide reasons and supporting evidence that highlights the importance of each of the habits. Each habit will delve into an example of how well-known people have demonstrated these traits followed by a guide on how to develop the traits for yourself through the Habit Formation Framework.

The best way to approach this chapter is to regularly return to it as you work your way through the book. At the conclusion of each chapter, return to this chapter and continue on to understand how to apply the learnings.

If you've come here after reading the introduction, jump ahead to the Creative Assessment Test now and complete it before moving forward. It's important to measure a baseline so you can track your own progress.

Habit Formation Framework

In his book *The Power of Habit*, Charles Duhigg described the *Habit Formation Framework*. As Duhigg explains, the framework is not a prescription but simply a way to understand how habits work and how we can change negative habits or to make positive ones stick.

Take solace in Duhigg's words: "Change might not be fast and it isn't always easy. But with time and effort, almost any habit can be reshaped."

At the essence of every habit are three components: **cue, routine** and **reward**.

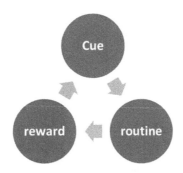

Figure 18: Process of habit formation

The *cue* is something that triggers and action. Repeating this action soon becomes a *routine*. And the reason the action is repeated is because you have attached some *reward* to this behavior.

To break this cycle down, the first thing you need to do is identify your routine. Perhaps in the early moments of the COVID-19 pandemic, to take a break from a project you're working, let's say, writing a research paper, your routine involved checking your phone in the afternoon to read the news —"Just for a few minutes," you tell yourself. Then, before you know it, you're elbows-deep in endless scrolling through news updates on your phone instead of working on your paper.

To diagnose what causes you to stick to this routine, you need to ask: what is the reward? What has created this loop in my mind that this action produces this reward? Perhaps the reward is in staying informed or in finding something new and interesting to discuss with family and friends, or just giving your mind a break. But the next day you feel terrible because your paper has not progressed. Despite the terrible feeling, you continue to stay glued to the news until the end of the day.

It can be tricky identifying the reward, as it's not always a simple equation of $A + B = C$. Experiment with several different rewards purely to test what was driving the routine of scrolling through the news all afternoon. Try going for a walk outside, reading a physical newspaper or magazine, watching a documentary on Netflix or YouTube, reading articles on sites like Mental Floss or Atlas Obscura, or reading only the updates on the World Health Organization website. Any of these activities may trigger the same reward sensation as scrolling through news sites.

Once you've identified your reward, you next want to identify the cue. What is it that triggers your desire to scroll through the news? Perhaps the cue is a certain time; the clock strikes three and you think, 'time to read the news!'

Here, then, are the three parts of your habit:

1. **Cue**: 3pm
2. **Routine**: Read the news until end of day
3. **Reward**: A break from your research paper

Once you've identified these three parts of your habit, you can now develop a new routine and reward cycle that the same cue triggers.

This process fits neatly with my six-step C-R-E-A-T-E process which, if you recall, is concept, raw materials, elements, atmosphere, thought excursions and execution. The initial cue that triggers us to embark upon the routine of the C-R-E-A-T-E process is identifying and recognizing that we have experienced a corona event. This event coerces us to reevaluate what values in life are most important to us. Our corona dilemma arises when we realize that we have a choice.

Figure 19: The Corona Dilemma

If we make the decision that we genuinely *want* to protect these newly established or reestablished values and to change the way we do things in life, then we need to engage in the C-R-E-A-T-E process. Our reward is in experiencing the pleasure and satisfaction that derive from coming up with creative ideas. If we succeed in transforming our concept through to execution through the C-R-E-A-T-E process then the reward of realizing our aspirations provides the positive reinforcement for us to do it again. And so the cycle continues.

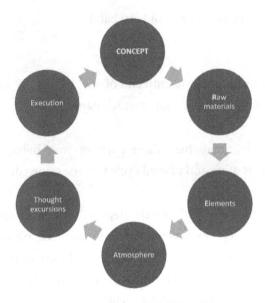

Figure 20: The C-R-E-A-T-E cycle

In this chapter, our focus is in developing creative habits. Duhigg's framework shows that you *can* change habits, but that it takes mindful, deliberate action to do so. The COVID-19 pandemic has allowed many of us to pause and take stock of many aspects of our lives, our work and career, our achievements, and what really matters most to us. And if we have faced the corona dilemma it has also given us the chance to reflect and to decide to make the changes we need to make. It has given us the perfect playing field upon which we can create our next normal. It will take work and effort and dedication, but on the other side is a life you want to lead.

Creative Assessment Test

In this section, I invite you to take a short test to identify the creative habits that we can hone.

Answer the following questions using the 1-to-10 scale below to rate your responses. As a cross-reference, ask a close friend or partner to answer these same questions about you to see how they think you match each of these items.

1. never
2. very rarely
3. rarely
4. infrequently
5. sometimes
6. occasionally
7. often
8. quite often
9. very often
10. always

Creative Assessment Test (CAT)

1. Do you challenge the status quo?
2. Are you curious about why things are the way they are?
3. Do you need space and time to feed your soul?
4. Do you focus intensely?
5. Do you think and speak in pictures and images?
6. If you are passionate about something will you see it through no matter what it takes?
7. Are you unconcerned of what other people think about what you do?
8. Do you have a mind that rarely slows down?
9. Do you feel deeply?
10. Do you sometimes think and behave like a child?

What did you score?

This test has been developed based upon extensive research in identifying the 10 most widely recognised and proven characteristics of people who have scored high in tests measuring divergent thinking and creative reasoning – that is, those who excel in 20-20 Thinking. The possible scores for this test range from 10 to 100. In a survey of 521 participants to whom this test was administered, across an age demographics ranging from 18 to 65-year old, the average score was 67.

If you scored less than 50 you are in roughly the bottom 5 percent of the population in terms of your level of creativity. Approximately two thirds of those surveyed scored between 60 and 73. If you scored 80 or more, you are high on the scale of creativeness, and in roughly the top 5 percent and probably don't need this book. It will probably not come as a surprise to you to know that those you scored in this top range (a score or 80 or more) came from a range of those areas and professions that we would normally associate with high levels of creativity. This group included an artist, a professional musician, a best-selling international author, highly successful business professionals and entrepreneurs, a brain surgeon, a Nobel Prize laureate and even a former High Court judge. But it may surprise you that included in this "elite" group were both undergraduate and high school students, a few individuals that classified themselves as "self-employed", a plumber (in-between jobs) and several people who fell into the occupation category of "domestic duties."

For the rest of us who scored less than 80, is the opportunity to hone those habits that will increase your creative prowess. You should start by focusing on developing those habits in which you scored 6 or less in the test. Here is some guidance in respect to the various distribution of scores.

10 – 49: If you're looking at being creative then there is much about you and your personality that needs changing. Or perhaps you can continue as an accountant.

50 – 59: If you focus on those questions in which you scored 6 or less then you'll soon be creating your way to a new life.

60 – 79:   With a little honing of your less creative traits you'll soon be a creative superstar.

80 – 100:   Give this book to someone who needs it.

Ten habits of highly creative people

The ten questions in the Creative Assessment Test (CAT) correspond to the ten habits identified through extensive research of the creative habits and traits of creative geniuses. Each subheading will begin with an overview of why this habit is important and end with a guide on how to begin developing the habit.

Although Duhigg's "Habit Formation Framework" may be readily applied to assist in the development of some of these habits, for some are more obscure habits the three components of cue, routine and reward will be less evident. In these instances you may consider that the cue to develop these habits is some aspect or component of the 20-20 Thinking process. For example, with Habit #3 Do you need space and time to feed your soul? the *cue* to initiating this habit is found in developing your "atmosphere" – the "A" in the C-R-E-A-T-E process. The *routine* you develop to support this habit will depend upon what your particular creative space looks like and how you go about creating the atmosphere to surround it. The *reward* for this habit – as with many of the 10 habits – is the satisfaction and elation related to creating a new idea.

Now let's take a look at our 10 habits.

Habit #1 Do you challenge the status quo?

Marina Abramovic is a Serbian conceptual and performance artist who continuously dreamed up new ways to perform and create emotionally moving art. You may have heard of her through her 2010 piece, *The Artist Is Present*, which was held at the Museum of Modern Art in New

York and subsequently went viral. In her performance, Abramovic sat silently at a wooden table; across from her is an empty chair where a person is invited to sit and lock eyes with her, allowing the artist to create an intimate connection with a stranger. Many of those who participated found themselves moved to tears. There was even a blog that ran called Marina Abramovic Made Me Cry!

Prolific, intriguing, and famous for crossing over to the mainstream—a rare feat in conceptual art—Abramovic was actually unknown to the art world for 40 years, a portion of which she spent living in obscurity and poverty in a van with her then partner. Her family also emerged from a country that now no longer exists, Yugoslavia, and she grew up in a home that was ran like a boot camp. If we're talking about change and crisis, we can learn much from Abramovic, from both her struggles and her eventual triumph. As she tells *The Guardian*,

> *"From a very early time, I understood that I only learn from things I don't like. If you do things you like, you just do the same shit. You always fall in love with the wrong guy. Because there's no change. It's so easy to do things you like. But then, the thing is, when you're afraid of something, face it, go for it. You become a better human being."*

With this thought, Abramovic was able to discover more about herself and create unique performance pieces. We can start small, with small discoveries. You can start with a list: What things do you want to change?

Change, by its nature, comes from messing up the established way of things, which can feel terrifying. The status quo has settled the way it has for a reason, and even if resistance to change isn't found within you it will likely be found externally. There are two questions that drive every creative person more than any others, they are, what if? and why not?

They question what everyone else takes at face value. While sometimes uncomfortable for those around them, the habit of challenging the way things are – especially during times of tumultuous change as we experienced in the COVID-19 pandemic – is what enables creatives to redefine the realms of what's possible.

So, this is what you need to do to develop this habit. For starters add the two sentences what if? and why not? to your vocabulary. Be on the lookout for seeing things you don't understand. When you let the water out of the kitchen sink after washing the dishes, notice that the water spirals down the sinkhole in a particular direction and ask yourself why. When the government tells you there is a need to sign up to a new app during the coronavirus pandemic question what that need is.

Though seen by many in society as a sign of weakness to ask questions and admit "I don't know", actually it requires a lot of confidence to submit to another. But the more you do it, the more questions you ask, the more creative you will become. Creativity grows with knowledge and you need constant fuel for the creativity fire. The more questions you ask, the brighter you are going to get, and the better ideas you are going to have.

Habit #2 Are you curious about why things are the way they are?

Habit 2 is actually the motivator to Habit 1; curiosity drives you to challenge the way things are. Creative people are insatiably curious and generally opt to live the examined life, and even as they get older, maintain a sense of curiosity about life. Whether through intense conversation or solitary mind-wandering as we do during our thought excursions, creatives look at the world around them and want to know why, and how, it is the way it is. As Albert Einstein once said, "I have no special talents. I am only passionately curious. The important thing is to not stop questioning." Curiosity has its own reason for existing.

Professor Wilma Koutsaal in a 2017 study published in *Psychology Today* looked into the connection between curiosity and creativity. Her study found that "general curiosity" (also called "diversive curiosity") is a form of curiosity associated with broad interests, directly leads to higher creativity. This is because those that are generally curious — meaning, those that enjoy learning new topics — like "information seeking", or reviewing all sorts of materials, even those that are only tangentially connected to the problem that needed solving. This means that their path to the solution is not a straight line. But wide information seeking, diverging from the path to follow off-roads and narrow alleys, leads to deeper "idea generation" and more creative problem-solving. These were the terms of the researchers who devised the study, but you can relate them to the creative triad in our own C-R-E-A-T-E framework. There is the *concept* that is the subject of our curiosity. "Information seeking" is analogous to gathering our bits of information or *raw materials* (recall-research-reach out) and "idea generation" refers to our *elements*.

How can you turn general curiosity into a habit? Perhaps before sticking to a single solution, it is best to spend time in collecting your raw materials. Recall concepts, research, and reach out to others and accept everything without prejudice, no judgment or dismissal – and no thinking "well, that's stupid! It's never going to work!" Simply take note of all of them, and you might just be surprised by the unique ideas or patterns that will emerge from the seemingly disconnected mess.

We must therefore be prepared to open ourselves to new experiences. Openness to experience – the drive for cognitive exploration of one's inner and outer worlds – is the single strongest and most consistent personality trait that reflects creative achievement. Research has found that the desire to learn and discover seems to have significantly more bearing on the quality of creative work than intellect alone. Daniel Kaufman says that creative people constantly shake things up – because they are curious. Diversity of experience, more than anything else, is critical to creativity, says Kaufman. Creatives like to experience new things and avoid anything that makes life more monotonous or mundane. "Creative people have more diversity of experiences, and habit is the killer of diversity of experience," says Kaufman.

So, if you want to boost your creativity, try out a new creative outlet or a totally different medium of expression, or take a new route home from work, or seek out a new group of people with different interests or values from those you keep. Openness to new experiences can help increase your integrative complexity – the capacity to recognize new patterns and find links among seemingly unrelated pieces of information. This awareness is vital for tapping into the currents of change within both yourself and the world around you. The world is changing, the COVID-19 pandemic is proof of that. But to the disinterested bystander this change is unpredictable and wild. When you are more curious about the world around you, the changes within it start to make more sense.

For that *intra*-personal change to become more curious of things around us and to challenge the status quo does not require a revolution. We can start small, as small as, "I want to change my route home from the gym." Do this once, then make notes by answering the following questions: What one new thing did you discover when you took a different path home – perhaps a café you haven't tried before or the alternate route was less congested? What one thing do you want to do or gain on this path next time? Maybe try a sandwich at the café? Speak to the barista? Bypass the traffic outside the school?

Do you like *who you are* on this new path? (Yes/No).

If you answer "Yes" to the last question, chances are high you will continue taking this path, and this will become your habit.

Now, try applying this process to something bigger: "I want to change my career path." See how you go.

Habits #3 Do you need space and time to feed your soul?

Hopefully you're well and truly considering the potential benefits that a changed environment may present. But as we learned in Chapter 2, to start changing the way we do things starts from within and requires individual or *intra*-personal change. One of the opportunities that a changed environment bestows upon us is the ability to change within yourself – to change our paradigms – and for this to happen we need to start thinking differently and to approach life from a new perspective. We discovered in Chapter 3 that 20-20 Thinking entails not being afraid to be alone with your thoughts and being open to the possibility that solitude can bring answers that we can't access when we are surrounded by people or otherwise distracted by the things around us.

Nurturing the development of your positive creative change works like growing a plant from a seed. You want to make sure you give your idea all the nutrients, the resources, the attention it needs. But you also need to be mindful not to overwater, to suffocate your creativity by overthinking and crowding your head with expectations. Giving yourself space and time is as much part of the process as sitting down and working through it. Consider what neurologist Vinod Deshmukh calls the "cognitive pause-and-unload" process, wherein we relax our minds and let go of old ideas or patterns of thought that bring us no closer to the solution. During this process – for example, when we're in the shower and suddenly get struck by an "a-ha!" moment – we become open to new ideas.

According to a Stanford study, walking is another form of mind relaxation and "cognitive pause" that can boost creative inspiration. Apple's Steve Jobs and Facebook's Mark Zuckerberg are known for holding meetings while walking or standing up instead of sitting down. More study needs to be done, as the researchers also assert, but the surprising thing is their finding that just the simple act of walking – not the environment per se – contributes to the boost of creativity. Says Marily Opezzo, one of the study's co-authors, "I thought walking outside would blow everything out of the water, but walking on a treadmill in a small, boring room still had strong results, which surprised me."

That surprised me too, but it's good news for us who crave for a pause in our day every now and then.

In Chapter 5 we explored various locations where your mind is more at ease and free to wander. We also found that an important aspect of finding your special "space" was to ensure that the atmosphere surrounding your location was devoid of distractions – especially the likes of cell phones and other smart devices. The other half of finding your "space-time oasis" is of course making the time to feed your soul? Many great artists have said that they do their best and most creative thinking either very early in the morning or late at night. For many creative people, waking up early is a way to avoid distractions. Ernest Hemingway woke up at 5 a.m. every day to begin writing. He said, "There is no one to disturb you and it is cool and cold and you come to your work and warm as you write." Vladimir Nabokov started writing immediately after he woke up at 6 or 7 a.m. and Frank Lloyd Wright made a practice of waking up between 3 and 4 each morning then working for several hours before heading back to bed. J K Rowling starts writing at 9 a.m. every morning. She says the earlier she starts writing, the more productive she is.

Not all creative minds are morning people. Franz Kafka routinely stayed up all night writing, and William Styron (author of Sophie's Choice, among other bestsellers) woke up at noon every day and considered his "morning" routine to be staying in bed for another hour to think. No matter when it is, individuals with high creative output will often figure out what time it is that their minds start firing up, and structure their days accordingly.

How do we develop this habit? For starters you have to be cognisant of what works for you in terms of both the space and time that best allows your mind to relax and wander. In order to be open to creativity, one must have the capacity for constructive use of solitude. One must overcome the fear of being alone. Remember *metacognition* – thinking about what you are thinking. Pay attention, and especially pay attention to what you pay attention to. Worry less about getting things done, and more about the worth of what you're doing. Is it those first few minutes after waking up, or when you are having a shower, or when you're walking the dog or when you're on the treadmill at the gym? Where and when your "space-time oasis" is matters less than what you do when you are there. Keep this time and place sacred to you. Enjoy *your* time of solitude and being alone with your thoughts. The feeling and revitalization of your soul will become the reward – but you have to give it time and space to let it happen.

Habit #4 Do you focus intensely?

With the previous habit we learned of the importance of relaxing the mind and letting go, but of course in order to get actual work done, or to materialize the solution to whatever concept we are working on, we need to develop our ability to intensely focus. Creative people get into what Kaufman calls the "flow state", which he defines as "the mental state of being completely present and fully immersed in a task."

Even if the phrase sounds novel, you have definitely been in this state before. Some people call it being "in the zone". Has anyone ever called your name several times while you were performing a task – for example, reading a book – and you didn't hear them? You were probably in the "flow state" then, so focused were you on the task at hand that every other sound or stimulus simply faded into the background. Think back to that time this happened to you: what made that task so special? You'll find that it's probably something that you enjoyed, but which also challenged you. To create something, to add something new to the world, you also need to find that task that equally enriches and challenges.

Of course, remember also the importance of upskilling. "[Creative people] have found the thing they love, but they've also built up the skill in it to be able to get into the flow state," says Kaufman. "The flow state requires a match between your skill set and the task or activity you're engaging in." If you want to get into the flow state of creating digital art, for example, you need to first develop the skills to do so, or else you won't be able to focus at all.

Highly creative people are energized by taking big mental leaps and starting new things. Things that excite them and things they can get fully emersed in. Existing projects can turn into boring slogs when the promise of something new and exciting is extinguished. In hindsight I feel that a major contributing factor as to why many of my creative ideas and projects never saw the light of day was that I lost interest at or during the "execution" phase – to me that was the linear, mostly mundane, and "boring" part of the creative process. For me, in many instances, I didn't have anyone – or at least anyone who was interested – to whom I could share my ideas or for simply "handing over" the project. But perhaps more relevantly, I didn't fully understand or appreciate the creative process and how each of the different phases were interrelated. Having subsequently developed the C-R-E-A-T-E process I can now see the errors of my way and where I went wrong.

Creative individuals understand the value of a clear and focused mind. Of course, intense focus requires that you limit distractions. Quite often creatives cannot multi-task effectively and it may take twenty minutes or so to re-focus after being interrupted, even if the interruption was a few seconds in taking a fleeting glance at an incoming message. Even the knowledge of an expecting message may be sufficient to distract you and hence derail the requisite level of focus. The late Maya Angelou, poet, civil rights activist, and Pulitzer Prize nominee would check into hotel rooms with sparse décor and write from 7 a.m. to 2 p.m. each day. This ensured that she had no distraction and could get into the "flow state" of creating her poetry. As with our previous habit, finding the right space and setting aside a definite period of undisruptive time is critical to the practice of intense focusing.

This is something you can try. Find a location where you won't be distracted. This could be a cafe, a library, or a cabin in the woods. Or, it could be your kitchen before the children get up. Set up this area as your "thinking" area where you can focus on your task at hand. Now remove the distractions. What is considered distracting differs between individuals, of course; some people can only work when there's music playing, while other people crave complete silence. So, take some time to think about this, and experiment with what works for you. But once you have exhausted your ability to continue to focus intensely – stop. Walk away and put your concept completely out of your mind. As you will see in Chapter 4, this is the time for your subconscious to do the heavy creative lifting.

Habit #5 Do you think and speak in pictures and images?

Most people think in words. People who don't think visually often have a hard time imagining the mental lives of those who do. When asked to imagine a traffic accident people who think in words come up with not very detailed descriptions, in comparison with people who are thinking in pictures. The ability to rationalize concepts and complex problems is enhanced through visualization. Picture thinkers don't have the distraction of converting words into images, they *think* in pictures. Picture thinkers are also called right-brainers but the question regarding about what goes on in our left and right brain hemispheres is a never-ending story and we will certainly not find the answer in this book. But what we do find is that people who think and speak in pictures and images are sometimes socially awkward. For instance, school systems are mainly auditory-sequential oriented and tend to favour those students that process information 'verbally'. Not surprisingly, we find that visual thinkers often encounter learning difficulties at school. Musk did, Einstein did as so too did many other creative individuals. But not only at school. Many visual thinkers don't fit well in society, traditional companies and institutions. They do things in other ways than expected or "normal", due to their "weaknesses" in thinking. But at the university of creativity – they graduate with first class honours.

In the past decade, cognitive neuroscientist Maria Kozhevnikov and her colleagues have found evidence to suggest that we need to move beyond simply categorizing people as either "visual" or "verbal" but rather consider the attributes of both mental processes. So while we may find support for the idea that creative people use the right hemisphere while people who are good at organizing things are using their left hemisphere we can also find support for the idea that creative and non-creative thinking are not necessarily two different things but are more reinforcing each other. So, this means that to learn to be creative we need to learn to practice both types of thinking – but exploring your concept *must* begin by initially visualizing what it looks like.

Albert Einstein has long been considered as a master of visual thinking, but few have examined in detail the way he described the thought process.

> "What, precisely, is 'thinking'? When, on the reception of sense impressions, memory, pictures emerge, this is not yet 'thinking.' And when such pictures form sequences, each member of which calls forth another, this too is not yet 'thinking.' When, however, a certain picture turns up in many such sequences, then – precisely by such return – it becomes an organizing element for such sequences, in that it connects sequences in themselves unrelated to each other. Such an element becomes a tool, a concept. I think that the transition from free association or 'dreaming' to thinking is characterized by the more or less preeminent role played by the 'concept'."

Re-read the above passage but now having reviewed the C-R-E-A-T-E process and the importance of your concept and the way in which the elements are created through our thought excursions. Could this be what Einstein was trying to describe when he was articulating the thought process?

Serbian-American inventor and futurist Nikola Tesla, who is celebrated for designing the AC (alternating current) electricity supply system and inventing the "Tesla coil" that we still use in radio technology today, was known to visualize ideas for months or even years before committing a single pencil line to paper. He called this period "the period of incubation" where he thinks about the problem "without any deliberate concentration."

Tesla was actively against rushing towards a solution. He first thought about the idea, turning it this way and that, before becoming more deliberate in his thinking, narrowing his mental investigation and zeroing in on a solution. He called this "the period of direct effort", where he would begin to feel that he was close to a solution, but knew that he just needed his subconscious mind to keep working at it. Tesla knew the power of visualization when he said, "The inventions I have conceived in this way have always worked." Harvard University researcher and psychologist Shelley Carson agrees with Tesla about this all-important "incubation period." In her book *The Creative Brain* she wrote:

> "Often one potential but unhelpful solution may block your ability to think up other solutions while the unhelpful one is still fresh in your mind. The incubation period, however, allows you time to forget inappropriate solutions upon which you may have become fixated. But you don't have to necessarily step away from a project to loosen up your mind, either."

Not everyone can be Tesla, whose visual ability was so acute that he was said to be able to provide measurements to craftsmen building his device even without a sketch. But we can all start by developing simple habits of visualizing our ideas and solutions. Dr Srini Pillay, writing for the *Harvard Health Blog*, said that research has shown that doodling, often considered a sign of distraction, can actually help you stay alert and attentive, improving your focus and allowing you to retain details even of a particularly boring lecture. Dr Pillay also says that doodling is a way to give your brain a break, as continuous attention can be a strain. A 30-minute reprieve can then help you concentrate more and fill in gaps in your thinking.

You can also use your doodles more deliberately. You can create mind maps, which are diagrams where ideas and the connections between ideas are presented visually. You can find software programs online that can help you create digital mind maps, but you can also go the traditional route using only a sketchpad and a pencil. To develop this habit, it might help to place a pad of paper and colored pencils near your "thinking" area. They can serve as your cue to begin sketching or doodling, especially when you get overwhelmed, or bored. Think of a reward that would incentivize you to keep sketching whenever this happens. Perhaps after 30 minutes of mind-mapping or doodling, you can tell yourself that your reward is an episode of your favorite show. Or perhaps even better, do something physical that will reward your brain for all the hard work it's done; go for a jog, walk the dog or even rake up the leaves in your backyard.

Unfortunately for many of us, and for some reason, visualization doesn't come naturally. We need to locate that muscle and strengthen it voluntarily. Just like going to the gym, it'll take considerable time and dedication to build a strong physique. Here is an exercise that can help us flex that visualization muscle.

Let's consider, for example, that you are feeling dissatisfied in your current job. You should have no difficulty in imagining what this looks like as you have done it for a long time. But now try and imagine this in your mind's eye – and see yourself at your workplace. If you feel your job is basically OK but there's a few things that really get to you about it, begin by imagining what your job would look like if these things were not there or were changed in a way to create a pleasurable environment. If this doesn't work or you feel you would prefer a new job entirely then focus on imagining yourself in this new workplace environment.

Either way the technique is basically the same. After relaxing into a deep, quiet and meditative state of mind, imagine you are working at your idyllic workplace environment. What does it look like? Who is there? What are you doing? Why are you happy? What is it that is satisfying you and what are the new or different things here that were not at your old job? Remember that the way we think and how we behave is influenced more by what we are afraid of, or concerned with, than what is pleasurable or comforts us (recall Maslow's Pyramid from Chapter 1). So, what then is *not* in this new workplace is most important. What is it that you can't see now but you *saw* when you visualized your current job? Was is that dropkick associate or your boss with bad breath? Or the constant distracting drone of the photocopier in the adjacent workstation? Try and get the feeling that in yourself this new workplace environment *is* possible and experience it as if it were happening now. In short, imaging it exactly the way you would want it to be – as if you were there now.

Repeat this thought excursion whenever you are in your "space-time oasis" or whenever you think about it and again perhaps when you are about to go to sleep. If your intention and motivation to make a change are clear and explicit, chances are good that this will lead to some type of shift happening at work. Give the power of visualization a chance to happen.

We've probably all read books that tell us to visualize our goals vividly – as if having achieved them already. If can you get your mind-muscle back in shape, you'll soon be able to see yourself being who you really want to be. With the power of visualization, you can change your habits, start new habits, or break bad habits. In a nutshell, you can apply visualization all areas of your life.

Habit #6 If you are passionate about something will you see it through no matter whatever it takes?

Are you familiar with the film, *Apocalypse Now?* Directed by Francis Ford Coppola and considered the greatest war film of all time, it was constantly at risk of not being finished. Its 238-day shoot was plagued with numerous production crises: Coppola dropping his original lead star, his new lead star Martin Sheen suffering a near-fatal heart attack, Coppola himself having an epileptic seizure, Marlon Brando turning up on set underprepared and with various demands (such as changing his character's name), and a typhoon destroying much of the film set. Coppola had to risk Inglenook, the vast property he bought from earnings from *The Godfather*, to finish this film.

Any other person without his passion and dedication would have just given up, but in the end, he finished his project that continues to mesmerize audiences with its power. And he still had Inglenook! As he tells *The Guardian* in an interview, "I never let not knowing how to do something stop me from trying to do it," he says. "I always got myself into those situations because it was exciting, and I got to do all these wonderful, nutty things."

It seems the difference between a career-defining triumph and a dismal failure came down to, like many a good film, a satisfying ending: Coppola's determination to see the film through to the end was ultimately what gave him something to be proud of. Think about how many projects could have been revered like Apocalypse Now but were abandoned unfinished when the challenge seemed to great. Sure, this book can show you how to generate revolutionary creative thoughts and ideas, but when the future is up for grabs in a post-COVID world, making a difference will be the domain of those who know how to follow through with their ideas.

The road to success is paved with failures. Lots of them. Doing things differently means you will probably do things badly or wrong; so expect that and don't let caution get in the way of creativity. For the creative the more ideas you generate, the greater chances you will produce an eventual masterpiece. But for the creative mind, every failure is a lesson, and a chance to innovate. As American inventor Thomas Edison once said, "I have not failed 10,000 times – I've successfully found 10,000 ways that will not work." To develop a light bulb that is commercially viable, Edison went through thousands of prototypes before finally finding the one design that did work.

Creative people are passionate about what they do. Whether they work as an artist or work at a bank, creative people strive to reach a successful outcome. They can come across as intense at times, but it stems from their passion to create something wonderful. Having confidence and trust in your abilities is also closely linked to the capacity to fail. If you are confident that you are on the right track, then you are more likely to be able to take criticism and negative feedback well and to learn from your mistakes. For a highly creative person, this ability to trust themselves, and to trust that they know what they are doing and to be able to perform each time, means that they can keep going, even when others are telling them to stop.

Once you have reassured yourself that what you are doing is worthwhile and that it *can* be done then it's a matter of having the perseverance and determination to stick with it. Monty Python co-founder John Cleese explained how he did this when writing scripts in his 1991 lecture on creativity.

> ▐▐ *"I was always intrigued that one of my Monty Python colleagues seemed to be more talented than I was but did never produce scripts as original as mine. And I watched for some time and then I began to see why. If he was faced with a problem, and fairly soon saw a solution, he was inclined to take it. Even though he knew the solution was not very original. Whereas if I was in the same situation, although I was sorely tempted to take the easy way out, and finish by 5 o'clock, I just couldn't. I'd sit there with the problem for another hour-and-a-quarter, and by sticking at it would, in the end, almost always come up with something more original. My work was more creative than his simply because I was prepared to stick with the problem longer."*

The next time you find yourself mentally exhausted, stick it out for a little longer. Developing the habit of finishing what you started can begin with a simple change of perspective. Some of us abandon our projects because we are more worried about what other people may think about what we are doing – and heaven forbid – the possibility of failure. But, again, it doesn't matter if you make a mistake or even fail, just as long as you learn from the experience for your next idea. I have always believed there are many things much worse that failure – not learning from them is the very worst.

So, to develop this habit of seeing something through to completion do the following. When you get to the stage of a project or trying to solve a problem and you start thinking things like "This is not going to work" or "It's time to give up" take the following challenge. Grab your pen and paper and start writing down the counter arguments for: But what if I succeeded?

- What have I learned from this situation?
- How can I grow as a person from this experience?
- What are three positive things about this situation?

And even if you *do* fail, as Coppola touched on above, what if the experience itself can be the reward?

Habit #7 Are you unconcerned of what other people think about what you do?

Often the greatest fear people have about doing new and different things is what other people may think of what they are doing. You can tell by now that habits 6 and 7 are intertwined: if you fear what others may think, you will not be able to finish what you have started. For some of us that peer pressure is too great that we are too afraid to even begin! Perhaps our ideas are too unusual, and we convince ourselves that this will *definitely* not take off. But remember that innovations *are* unusual – if they've existed before, they wouldn't be called innovations.

Creative individuals would rather be authentic than popular. Staying true to who they are, without compromise, is how they define success even if means being misunderstood or marginalized. Take as an example the story of American composer Lin-Manuel Miranda and his hit Broadway musical, *Hamilton*. While reading a biography of Alexander Hamilton, one of America's founding fathers, Miranda had the idea of telling the story through hip-hop music, blending modern musical forms with classical theatre.

That is a bizarre idea, and it was ridiculed at first. When Miranda premiered a few songs to the Obamas at the White House in 2009, *The Daily Show's* Jon Stewart said on his show the next day, "You're rapping about Alexander Hamilton?!? This is kind of ridiculous." But Miranda stuck with his idea, working long hours: spending a day perfecting two lines of a song, and spending a full year writing the second song of the musical. His hard work and persistence paid off. *Hamilton* premiered in 2015 and was the most successful Broadway opening of all time. It has since won a Pulitzer and 11 Tonys, and Miranda himself was awarded a Genius Grant by the MacArthur Foundation. But you can tell that this was no overnight success. It was a grueling process of failures and disappointments, but a process that Miranda stuck with. He continually persevered, laughing in the face of criticism, because he knew that his idea was worth pursuing, even if no one else agreed.

I remember one time when I was playing golf with a work colleague at a rather prestigious, private golf course. It was a steamy hot summer afternoon and we were on the back nine and along way from the clubhouse. Then almost without warning we were hit by a sudden thunderstorm and the heavens opened. I was fortunate in that I had borrowed my wife's golf buggy and knew she always carried a foldable umbrella in her buggy. Without hesitation I grabbed the umbrella. My colleague was less fortunate so I offered refuge under my umbrella. He smiled at me and said, "I wouldn't be seen dead with *that* umbrella." I was startled then realized his reaction must have had something to do with the fact that the umbrella was bright pink. I, subconsciously thinking function over form, had really not even noticed its color. "So you'd prefer to get wet rather than be seen under a pink umbrella? I said. "In fact" he replied, "I'd prefer to get drenched and catch pneumonia." But the really scarry bit was that I think he was more than half serious.

John Cleese also believes that we shouldn't worry what other people think of what you're doing. "You've got to risk saying things that are silly and illogical and wrong, and the best way to get the confidence to do that is to know that while you're being creative, nothing is wrong" says Cleese, as "Nothing will stop you being creative so effectively as the fear of making a mistake." And as Aristotle once said, "There is only one way to avoid criticism: do nothing, say nothing, and be nothing."

One of the things I've learned over the years is that some of my ideas are more useful than others, and some, well, are simply too weird to try. Perhaps you need not spend a year writing a song (well, if you have the inclination, why not!) or getting off the ground that crazy invention you've always talked about, but you can develop the habit of not being afraid of what others may think. Vanessa Loder on *Forbes* provides various proven strategies, one of which connects to our Habit #5: visualizing or thinking in images. "Positive thinking alone is not enough. Research has shown that the best outcomes are created when we balance positive thinking with visualizing the future obstacles and struggles we will encounter," she writes.

When we worry about what other people are thinking, we steal valuable energy and confidence from ourselves and we start to doubt who we are and what we do is good enough. Remember, most people most of the time aren't paying much attention. They spend more time thinking about themselves than thinking about others. Perhaps we wouldn't worry so much about what people thought of us if we knew how seldom they did. Of course, we should have some concern about our image and self-esteem in what we do and what people think of us, especially if we want to be 'socially' accepted. However, there have been times when I've over-worried about this. Let's face it people are going to think what they are going to think and it's more their problem than yours unless you make it your problem. However, if it is a friend or family member, or someone else close to you, then it's probably a good idea to ask what's on his or her mind. Perhaps we should do as Dr. Seuss suggests: "Be who you are and say what you feel, because those who mind don't matter and those who matter don't mind."

So my best advice on how you can develop this habit is by limiting the amount of people that you should take notice of. The next time you have reservations about what you intend to do begin by asking yourself the following three questions:

1. Is this someone I hold in high regard?
2. Do I feel this person has my best interests at heart?
3. Are they giving me their opinion in an area in which they're knowledgeable?

If the answer to any of the questions above is "no", then you shouldn't be concerned with what that person thinks. If the answer to all three of these questions is "yes", then you should take that person's opinion into consideration. Nonetheless, always keep in mind that – at the end of the day – the opinion that matters most when it comes to you is your *own*. After all, no one knows you as well as you know yourself. You must make a conscious effort to let go what other people think. It's a skill that needs to be practiced, like meditating. But once you truly understand how to let go, you will see the world as entirely different.

Habit #8 Do you have a mind that rarely slows down?

The creative mind is a non-stop machine fueled by intense curiosity. There is no pause button and no way to power it down. This can be exhausting at times, but it is also the source of some crazy fun activities and conversations. If you're in a relationship with a highly creative person you probably already realize that their mind rarely slows down – and even when it does it's still wandering in search of more information. They're multi-tasking up until the moment they go to bed, and sometimes it keeps them awake at night.

The world is a creative person's oyster – they see possibilities everywhere and are constantly taking in information that becomes fodder for creative expression. As Henry James is widely quoted, a writer is someone on whom "nothing is lost." Writers will understand how people speak and painters will understand how people move. They take in their surroundings and draw inspiration from anything and everything around them. New experiences and changed environments, as we have experienced during the coronavirus pandemic and its aftermath, are real opportunities for creative people, novel situations and more inspiration to draw on.

But with a mind that rarely slows down doesn't necessarily equate to a frantic and chaotic lifestyle. Let's face it none of our minds *really* stop as they are constantly crunching the countless things we experience. While the average person's mind eventually stops thinking of ideas, unknown scenarios and possible outcomes, a creative person tends to dwell in their thoughts about the same. The main difference here is what creative people *do* with the things they are thinking of. As Jean-Luc Godard said it's not where you take things from – it's where you take them to that's important to the process of creating.

Thinking and mind wandering isn't valuable unless you're focusing on the right things, things that excite you or add value to your life. In the pre COVID-19 rush of everyday life, it was easy to lose sight of those things, or not even realize that they're already there, captured in the vast vaults of both your conscious and unconscious mind. By focusing on the C-R-E-A-T-E process and adding a little bit of structure and context to your daily routine you can make the most of all your mind's wanderings. It can help shift your perspective and align your thoughts to your concept, revealing things that you may have been looking for all along.

Before COVID-19 caused many cities and countries to go into lockdown and isolation, you may have been too busy to realize just how much your mind loves to wander. Many of us may have considered letting our minds wander a complete waste of time, so we filled our downtime with a multitude of external distractions both inside and outside of the house. Little by little, the noise and speed of the world have increased, so that we can hardly remember an era of slowness and quiet, when we could let our minds wander and think about what they wanted to think about, when we had time to consider where we were going and what we believed in.

The coronavirus pandemic and the lockdown, however, changed all this. With many workplaces shut down, with restaurants and movie theaters and department stores closed, now that many of us spend the 24 hours of each day sequestered in the sanctuary of our homes, suddenly we find ourselves alone with our thoughts. Even those for whom working from home and flexible work arrangements were possible, additional free time has been created because there were no more stressful daily commutes and no one timing your comings and goings of the day and no more running down the clock just because you "finish" at 5 p.m. but you've had nothing to do for the last half hour.

Mind-wandering, daydreaming, and thinking that arises from boredom, is at the heart of creativity. Mary Mann, author of *Yawn: Adventures in Boredom*, explained in a 2020 article in *The Atlantic* that people surveyed in Italy at the end of March 2020, had identified boredom as the most challenging part of isolation. She stated that "this annoying feeling is actually a sophisticated alert system, a sort of inner (and free!) life coach tapping us on the shoulder to suggest that we might want to change something."

Numerous recent studies in neuroscience have shown that daydreaming and mind-wandering can have a wide range of positive effects including; self-awareness, creative incubation, improvisation and evaluation, memory consolidation, autobiographical planning, goal driven thought, future planning, retrieval of deeply personal memories, reflective consideration of the meaning of events and experiences, simulating the perspective of another person, evaluating the implications of self and others' emotional reactions, moral reasoning, and reflective compassion.

A 2012 study headed by Daniel Levinson and published in the *Psychological Science* titled "The Persistence of Thought: Evidence for a Role of Working Memory in the Maintenance of Task-Unrelated Thinking" found that daydreaming can allow your brain to make connections you wouldn't normally make. Remember "R" (for raw materials) in our creative triad (C-**R**-E)—recall, research and reach-out. Daydreaming allows us to *recall* those bits of information we didn't even know were just floating around in our head, information that can lead to a bright idea – the formation of an element – or a solution to a problem or our concept we are working on.

So, what should we do to make the most of a mind that rarely slows down? At home, time and space have opened up in our minds. With more quiet time, more privacy, more stillness, we have an opportunity to allow our minds to wander and think about who we are, as individuals and as a society. Like so many of us, I have had the chance let my mind wander during times of home isolating. But such self-reflection, such tending to the inner self, should not be a onetime event. It should be an ongoing part of, what Henry David Thoreau calls, "a life lived deliberately." And that deliberate living requires an enduring change of lifestyle, paradigms and habits. At some point, the coronavirus will pass, or at least recede into the haze of other viruses and ailments. There has already been overwhelming suffering and loss of life, enormous economic devastation. The tragedy cannot be overstated. For years, we will be trying to rebuild the broken world. But perhaps the slower lifestyle in these times of isolation can help put the pieces back together. And perhaps a more contemplative, deliberate way of living can become permanent.

Recall the habit formation framework and consider how we can make meaningful thinking and daydreaming a habit. I mean healthy daydreaming, as there is such a thing as maladaptive daydreaming that interferes with your daily life. We don't want that!

Your routine would be taking a break from intense thought or activity and letting your mind wander. Perhaps your cue can be just the frustration stemming from not immediately finding an answer. This requires a high degree of emotional self-awareness as well. Are you getting frustrated? Are you feeling stuck? Then perhaps it's time to daydream. Your reward can be a brilliant idea you didn't even know was just waiting there to be discovered.

Habit #9 Do you feel deeply?

As you can see in our previous habit and with habit #3, creativity entails not being afraid to be alone with your thoughts and being open to the possibility that solitude can bring answers that we can't access when we are surrounded by people and are distracted. It is also interesting how in previous examples, the solution often lies not only in intense, focused thought but also in times when our mind is more at play and we are relaxed. Creativity is about human expression and communicating deeply. It's impossible to give what you don't have, and you can only take someone as far as you have gone yourself. A writer once told me that an artist must scream at the page if they want a whisper to be heard. In the same way, a creative person must feel deep if they are to communicate deeply.

Highly creative people, because they feel deeply, often can quickly shift from happiness to sadness or even depression. Their sensitive heart, while the source of their brilliance, is also the source of their suffering. As we have learned in Chapter 5 forcing yourself to try and be creative is a great way to kill creativity. We already take in so much information, sometimes the best thing to do is to take your mind off the problem and let the solution find you. Great ideas need time and space, however counterintuitive that might feel. When we are feeling deeply regarding a particular issue or concern, we have the ability to see "inside" the problem and often stumble upon a solution or new idea. The "a-ha!" moment is accompanied by the most amazing feeling. Think back to the last time you found a solution to a problem, be it tangible (how to fix a broken appliance) or abstract (the proposition you develop in your assignment). What did you feel? Happiness. Elation. All positive emotions, right? But now, as Kaufman rightly asks in his article in the *Harvard Business Review*, think back to what you felt *before* this creative insight.

I can almost see you wincing. Let me guess: anxiety? Worry? Frustration? All three?

These are negative emotions, but they didn't stop you from trying to solve the problem, did they? Why?

If we think back to our C-R-E-A-T-E process and the continuous creative triad cycle of; concept – raw materials – elements, we realize that it is essentially just a process for "connecting the dots." For sensitive people – those who feel deeply and have a heightened sensitivity to their surroundings and also an intensified experience of sensory input, like for sound, lighting, and scent – experience a world in which there are both more dots and more opportunities for connection. This type of sensitivity can be both a blessing and a curse, leading to a greater intensity of experience as well as emotional overwhelm. Journalist Andrea Bartz wrote in *Psychology Today* that "those who learn to dial down the relentless swooping and cresting of emotion that is the almost invariable accompaniment to extreme sensitivity are able to transform raw perception into keen perceptiveness."

So, rather than trying to harden yourself, you may want to harness your sensitivity into creative expression, so you too can learn to relate more to your inner feelings. This brings us to the emotion we need to harness to develop this habit: desire. As Kaufman argues, citing research in behavioral psychology, the characteristic that influences attention and stimulates creativity is "motivational intensity", defined as:

> *"How strongly you feel compelled to either approach or avoid something. For example, pleasant is a positive emotion, but it has low motivational intensity. In contrast, desire is a positive emotion with high motivational intensity."*

Kaufman describes desire here as a positive emotion, but we know from experience that desire also gives birth to negative emotions like frustration and hopelessness. But perhaps we should set aside this positive-negative dichotomy and embrace all of these emotions and understand that all of them are *useful* emotions that will propel us to our success.

For a concluding exercise to assist in developing this habit, write down the three most pressing desires you have, then write the emotions that you think you will feel as you try to fulfill these desires. Then visualize how you will overcome them.

Habit #10 Do you sometimes think and behave like a child?

To a child, everything is new and filled with possibility. We shed this childlike wonder as we grow older, becoming world-weary and cynical. But regaining this sense of childlike wonder, of having fun, of embracing whimsy, is key to a creative life. Dr. Stuart Brown, author of the play: *How It Shapes the Brain*, founded a not-for-profit organization called the National Institute for Play which focused on inspiring adults to regain this sense of wonder. Dr. Brown also applied this objective to his own life, turning moments that can be frustrating into a moment of fun. For example, once he lined up at a pharmacy where there was a long queue. Instead of feeling irritated, he decided to talk to the other people waiting in line with him and enjoy the conversation. Simple as this may sound it completely changed how he felt. In his research, he found that those who don't make time to play are more prone to depression, and that play has an active presence in the accomplishments of successful people.

British comedian John Cleese agrees that the most creative people have this childlike facility to play.

> **▌▌** *"You become the best in your field, when your work is your play", when your work is your play, you are like a child, out in the garden, having a great time picking flowers, creating castles and games out of beautiful imaginations; fulfilment is found when you let go of all inhibitions that cages and suffocates to death, creativity that's not discovered, life is better and its essence is discovered, when you refuse to be a copycat."*

The world deserves creative ideas that aren't afraid to be fun, even if it means being a bit childish. In the same way, the world's creatives deserve to have fun. If that's childish, then I guess we're all just big kids after all. And this is no new revelation. Chinese Confucian philosopher, Mencius (Meng-Tse) back in the 4th century BCE said "Great is the human who has not lost his childlike heart." Children have the creative quality but seem to lose it as they're told — "it's not the done thing". As Pablo Picasso once said, "Every child is an artist. The problem is how to remain an artist once he grows up." We must always be open to creativity, Children have it in their blood. If you agree with me then the problem becomes; How to remain truly creative after growing up? It shouldn't be just about the artists or musicians in the room, but about everyone. Engineers and programmers need to be creative in solving and writing their code, corporations must be the first to support the creativity of everyone who works with them to solve problems and all other roles – copyrighters, marketers, entrepreneurs. The automated and highly structured process we find in most businesses that eases our work and makes us more efficient in what we are doing doesn't mean obtaining the best results. We may become more efficient at a sub-optimal process.

According to British comedian Ricky Gervais the secret to keeping that creative mind is to never grow up. It isn't about becoming an adult without responsibility, just having enough time to play – the fool, goad, shock, laugh! Stumble on something that doesn't exist, try something, and don't be afraid to fail. Failure is also useful, it's just another adult blocker that needs to be overcome. As Einstein once said: "Creative thinking isn't synonymous with safe thinking, yet we forget to take risks when trying to come up with truly great ideas." A child faces risks, says what they think, don't make pre-judgments, and asks questions. The way they play, explore, and see the world doesn't have our adult concept of failure in mind, and time works at a different pace for them. Learning to overcome our fears, slow down, and be curious — a shift to that mindset — makes us more open and receptive and therefore more creative.

Openness to experience is one of the greatest correlations with a creative mindset. This was found in a trial conducted by psychology professors Darya Zabelina and Michael Robinson with undergraduate students who were instructed to imagine their classes had been cancelled for just one day. They had to present a text about what they'd do during that day. The only difference was — half of them would have to write, assuming they were 7 years old. Before they had time to finish the text, they were interrupted and had to take a Torrance Test of Creativity. The results showed those who had to think as children achieved better results. One of the study's conclusions was that the opportunity to play and explore can facilitate creative performance and originality. "The mindset of adults, on the other hand, is likely to involve trying to find the 'correct' conventional solution to a presented task or problem."

Remember the last time you were in a meeting with at least one half-decent idea in your mind, but you never spoke up? This is our fear of what others think or of being ridiculed. We need to overcome this feeling, to have this childlike mentality. Michael Dunn who lectures in business psychology at the University of Derby says "To be creative, what we're looking for isn't one idea, but dozens of ideas – some good, some average and some rubbish. We need to go through the wrong stuff to get to the right stuff. So, no matter how wild, wacky an idea is, we need to learn to suspend judgment and get it to the table. Children aren't bothered about doing that, they have no fear of saying what they think."

Here are a few tips on how may begin to acquire the habit of acquiring a childlike mindset at work or in your everyday life.

1. Imagine how a child would deal with the problem

Creatives long to see through the eyes of a child and never lose a sense of wonder. For them, life is about mystery, adventure, and growing young. Everything else is simply existing, and not true living. Think of yourself as a young child for a while — what would you do? Where, who, why, and how would you go, see, stay, and perform? To truly experience the difference between adult and children, take a walk with a two-year old. They see things you don't even notice. The French poet Baudelaire was right: "Genius is nothing more nor less than childhood recovered at will." Observing children in imaginative play reveals a wellspring of natural-born creativity. When engaged in pretend play, children take on multiple perspectives and playfully manipulate emotions and ideas.

2. Rethink problems without limits and rules

Children don't think in limits, they're chaotic. A child's imagination is unrestricted by the rules, it's free to go anywhere. When you need to be creative, you may not spend the whole day thinking conventionally as an adult, task oriented. Somewhere on your way to adulthood, you lost your innocence and assumed certain things couldn't be done or achieved. You were brought up like everyone else to think and see the world in the same way. We need to turn on your childlike mindset to facilitate creative originality as their world has no obstacles or rules. Children explore understandings that no adult would ever consider.

You need to regain that spontaneity again, make an effort to mentally suspend rules and conventions, to open yourself up to more possibilities.

So, question everything as children are always looking for answers. Get much more than a few answers to a question. And if your answers are limited by "this is how we always do it" or "this is how things are done", find something else. Think about how other people created services like Uber or Airbnb, or products – Steve Jobs used to question engineers as a child several times, insisting on more detailed questions to create a phone that should have only one main button, the iPhone.

3. Slow down and get bored

I'm sure we can all recall that pitiful lament: "Mum! I'm bored." Well, these days we just don't say it enough. When we're not working, we're doing our chores, watching TV, or Facebooking our friends, we just don't allow ourselves any proper downtime anymore. Allow yourself adequate downtime – remember your space-time oasis. It seems an impossible task nowadays, when we aren't working, watching TV or browsing our social media – but we need to create space to invoke possibilities. Our routine processes are executed quickly and with little effort, due to our experience of having gone through this before. At work, if you can't slow down for a long time, try to stop just a few minutes, as new alternative approaches may emerge. According to psychologist Martin Lloyd-Elliot "We need to make time and space to daydream, to meditate, to let our minds wander. Children embrace dead space and time and fill it with imagination. The greatest creative ideas often emerge from the gloom of boredom."

4. Look around

Give up control and look at things from a new angle. Children explore everything and play with their imaginations around what they see and touch. Change your habits, break your routine and occupy different spaces. Try a different route home or using other means of transport. Does it take more time? Even better! Or try strolling through a different park, sitting in a different part of a different café or pub, or exploring different markets for your products or services. These are all actions you can perform differently in your daily life.

To conclude with this – my favourite – habit I'd like to leave you with a few quotes for you to think about. Ernest Hemingway insightfully once said, "The thing is to become a master and in your old age to acquire the courage to do what children did when they knew nothing. " And how could I omit the quote attributed to two contemporaneous Irish wits, George Bernard Shaw and Oscar Wilde, when they proclaimed, "Youth is wasted on the young." But finally, and possibly the most appropriate closing quote for a book on how to develop new ideas, comes from British-American anthropologist Ashley Montagu when he proposed, "The idea is to die young as late as possible."

A Concluding Comment: So Where to From Here?

Congratulations for having stuck with it and made it to here. You have read about the importance of change as a medium for presenting opportunities. And everyone on the planet is acutely aware that our world has changed almost beyond recognition since 2020 when the coronavirus upended our lives. Hopefully you also amassed the courage and motivation to take on the corona dilemma challenge and realized there are different ways in which you can negotiate your next normal.

If there is one thing, above all else, that I hope to have conveyed to you in this book it's the realization that you – *and only you* – have the ability to make things better. All things and everything. Hopefully the concepts and tools I have presented will be the catalyst to ignite within you a renewed sense of purpose in life. Life's simply too short not to live it the way you want – the way you *really* want.

But as a word of caution, upon reading this book, do not expect to become creative – or perhaps more creative – overnight. The adage "old habits die hard" rings very true. English economist John Maynard Keynes once proclaimed the difficulty in creating your own creativity lie not so much in developing new ideas as in escaping from old ones. You have unwittingly dedicated almost your entire adult lifetime to becoming non-creative so be patient and retain the willpower it takes to achieve your goals and turn your concepts into reality.

So now it's up to you, take the tools and concepts you've learnt in this book and start planning how you can set about creating a future that will protect your re-established values and everything else in life that is important to you. Read – think – visualise – act. Learn how to rid yourself of your anti-creative habits and replace them with those that promote creative expression that derives from 20-20 Thinking.

And finally remember, every single new idea created has the ability to change your life and indeed, to change the world. In fact one single idea is the only thing that ever has.

ACKNOWLEDGEMENTS

In our world of rapidly advancing technology, ubiquitous social media, and an unrelenting global pandemic, never before have feelings of helplessness and self-worth been more prevalent. Since the onset of COVID-19, the question of how the human mind deals with change has now assumed a heightened significance. The issues raised and questions posed in this book seek to explore the workings of our mind in a time of change but in so doing, provide useful solutions. I have always been of the firm belief that in order to create something that is useful, one must go to the source of where it is to be used.

A publication such as this which seeks to serve a practical need necessarily benefits from the input of practitioners. As a general acknowledgement, I am greatly indebted to the work of those before – the scientists, the psychologists and the authors – that have attempted to answer this question, and to whom I have respectively acknowledged their contributions throughout this book.

I would particularly like to acknowledge Rebekah Oliver, who is currently studying law at the University of Sydney, for her invaluable input in the area of thought processes. Also I would like to acknowledge Kate Woodbury, a student of the arts and aspiring author, who brought to this publication her fresh, open-minded worldview to help us understand how to visualise and deconstruct our paradigms. To arts and law student Liam Slabber, who is passionate about creative writing and music, for his contribution in researching remodelling into the way we participate in creative spaces as we move toward our next normal.

Also a special acknowledgement to filmmaker Alexander Peter Lercher for providing invaluable input, especially with his special contribution to the "execution" phase of this book. I would also like to acknowledge the work of Sam King, an emerging writer and current student of a Master of Creative Writing course, who provided invaluable insight into creative processes. Special thanks also for the input by doctorate candidate, Eliza Victoria who assisted with research for this project, particularly around habits that drive creativity. I also gratefully acknowledge the contribution of Joshua Wallis, an arts/law student, whose assistance in reimagining the title's formulation for applied creativity in a post-COVID world was greatly valued.

In researching this book I have interviewed many creative individuals across all walks of life. I am deeply indebted by the wisdom shared with me by the Hon Michael Kirby, former Justice of the High Court of Australia, in explaining how creativity, when applied to the interpretation of the law, can provide for more humane and just outcomes. And a very special thanks to Dick Smith, a man of many talents; entrepreneur, adventurer, philanthropist and many more. Former Australian of the Year and world-breaking aviator, but when interviewed Dick did not consider himself as being a creative person and yet, to me, he personifies the very essence of creativity: "That's just who I am." To Professor Charlie Teo, neurosurgeon, researcher, educator, mentor and a world pioneer in minimally invasive keyhole neurosurgery. His thoughts and comments upon why people are unwilling to adapt to change were insightfully valuable.

Also a big thank you to Jason Swiney and the team at Fontaine Publishing for their incredible assistance during the production phase and in coming up with such a creative cover design. To Mark Roeder, international best-selling author, for his encouragement in making this book happen and to Anne Reilly – editor extraordinaire – whose initial review really assisted in getting me on the right path and in motivating me with her suggesting it would be "impossible" to publish in 2020. To Amin, Fallon and Amalina and all the crew at Avlaw for their obliging accommodation in letting their boss "do his thing."

And, of course, a huge and most sincere thank you to Colette Smith, who was relentless in her provision of extraordinary editing skills and in guiding this publication to the finishing line. Her amazing contribution of the introduction – with the clarity and insight of an eremitic scholar – set the scene for the message in this book.

Colette would also like to thank the Smith family for always encouraging her to explore and pursue her passions. A particular note of gratitude to Gordon, Kathryn, Arithon, and Calidore Smith, who selflessly, and at a moment's notice, opened their home to her at the start of the pandemic. Without this safety and security of home and family during such tumultuous times, she would not have had the clarity of mind nor ability to tackle a project such as this. She would also like to thank Brooke, Greg, Mia, and Dexter Robinson, who have likewise not only shown the kindness of opening their home to her during a pandemic, but also of giving her the gift of being her second family. Most of all, Colette wishes to thank her husband, Conor Curlett, whose enduring patience, kindness, rationality, understanding, and support never wavers – even across oceans in the midst of a pandemic.

Last but not least to Diane – my soul mate and everything else in life that is important. Without her enduring and selfless support over the past quarter of a century, this publication, and every other good thing in life, would never have happened.

Without the assistance and efforts of these people, this book would not have been possible, and while their contributions were invaluable, any errors or omissions are all of my own doing.

Finally, for those interested in further information on the subject of creativity, you may find some interesting information and reference materials at www.20-20thinking.com or ask questions of the author at www.thecoronadilemma.com.

ABOUT THE AUTHOR

Ron Bartsch BA, BSc, LLB, LLM, MPhil, DipEd, ATPL

 Ron is a social and media commentator and presents widely at international forums. He is considered one of the world leading authorities in aviation law and risk management and has been a published author for the past 25 years with over 10 books to his credit and with sales in excess of 10,000 units. Ron is the founder and Chair of Avlaw, an international consultancy firm, and formerly was the Head of Safety at Qantas Airways and Manager of Airline Operations with the Australian Civil Aviation Safety Authority.

Ron was admitted as a barrister to the High Court of Australia in 1993 and served as a presiding member of the Federal Administrative Appeals Tribunal until 2017. As a former high school mathematics and science teacher and also an experienced commercial pilot with in excess of 7,000 flying hours and ratings on over 30 multi-engine aircraft types including command endorsements on the Beechjet and Boeing 717. He has formal qualification in law, education, science and the arts. Ron is a director of Rex Airlines and visiting professor at several universities around the world.

In his spare time Ron plays keyboard with his aging rock buddies in Judge Jeffries, regularly gets beaten by his wife (in golf), jogs daily and takes his rescue dog Teddy for long walks to clear both their minds. Ron can be contacted through the website at: www.TheCoronaDilemma.com

INDEX